# A Joke
# a Day

## Simon Gibson

**All proceeds to Alzheimer's Research UK**

Published in 2014 by:

Stellar Books LLP
Dunham Gatehouse
Charcoal Road
Bowdon
Cheshire
WA14 4RY

www.stellarbooks.co.uk
ISBN: 978-1-910275-00-9

Illustrations by Paul Fisher.
Designed by Kate Bates.

We all need humour in our lives and Simon's hilarious book, *A Joke A Day*, promises plenty of laughter. Within moments of turning the pages, I had a big smile on my face – it's amazing how a joke can brighten the day and help us cope with difficult situations.

This is Simon's first venture into writing and it came about quite by chance. His ambitious plan to post a daily joke on Facebook for a whole year was intended to make his friends and family laugh and smile every day. When asked what he intended to do with this mirthful collection of material, the idea for the book grew – and now it's a highly amusing reality.

But there's a serious side to all this humour: by buying a copy of *A Joke A Day*, you are also helping Simon's chosen charity, Alzheimer's Research UK, to defeat dementia. All of the net proceeds from book sales are being donated towards our pioneering dementia research, bringing us closer to finding the preventions and new treatments so desperately needed. Our goal is to defeat dementia through research and *A Joke A Day* will help us fund more world class science to rid the world of this devastating condition. We are determined to have the last laugh on dementia!

**Rebecca Wood**
Chief Executive, Alzheimer's Research UK,
the UK's leading dementia research charity

**www.alzheimersresearchuk.org**

## A few words of thanks...

Whenever I read all the people being thanked in a book, I skip past if it is too long. Maybe everyone really does have hundreds of people to thank ... I have a dozen, by name, apart from, of course, all the FB friends (many of whom I know read, laughed and never either commented or 'liked' online – your omnipresent support made the year fly by).

Firstly, the five major supporters who contributed so much financially (and as it happens in other ways throughout the year) to make this book a reality:

Ian Green
Anthony Jones
Katy Baxter
Henry Saltmarsh
David Batchelor

Deidre Sanders, for pulling strings

Next, those that helped create the finished article from a stream of words and 'visions':

Kate Bates, who has donated hours to get the look of the book right. Paul Fisher, likewise, wielding his pens into the early hours, and who will be, forever, 'Frank'.

Now, the really personal bit:

My Dad, from whom, as far as we ever get our sense of humour from one person, I got mine. Jenny, my amazing wife, who puts up with being the but(t) of my jokes, just not usually online. Grace, Alice and Guy, all of whom could already get work as professional critics.

Finally, my love of comedy, of humour, is life long, and though I can honestly rarely recall who said what, I know that influences herein include comedians from the truly great Ken Dodd to Milton Jones, from Jimmy Carr to Tommy Cooper. If you like a laugh, or at least a smile, or maybe a groan (read the book!!), please find it in your heart to spend just £10.

 This indicates that as far as I know, I originated the joke/limerick concerned.

I always knew, one day, I would be a paperback writer. So:

Dear Sir or Madam, will you please buy (and read) my book,
It took me one year to write, will you take a look.
There are limericks and jokes, but none by Lear,
And I have a job, so have no fear.

If it sells three copies, then I won't have won,
But that won't change the fact it's been great fun!
It's a hundred pages give or take a few,
I've been writing for weeks, actually, 52.

Some jokes are mine, many more are repeated;
I'm telling you up-front so you won't feel cheated.

There's a cause here too, which I hope is OK –
I am raising money for ARUK.
I have friends and family that suffer now,
Alzheimer's isn't fun; you knew that? WoW.

So the plan is very simple, please take a look,
Then get out a tenner, and buy this book.
Every penny made goes to charity;
Yes, not a single one will come to me.
So please, please help me (there's a song in there);
If nothing else, you are now more aware.

Alzheimer's is tough, and there's a fight to be had;
So help with the battle, if only for Dad.

**Simon Gibson, March 2014**

# How it all started

**Simon Gibson**
January 1 near Thatcham, England via mobile

I have written a song for the New Year - it is all about a tortilla - if I am honest, it's more of a wrap ...

Like · Comment · Promote · Share                    👍 12  💬 3

## Quickly followed by:

**Simon Gibson**
January 2 near Newmarket

OK, OK, the demand has become too much, I WILL post 365 jokes on FB this year. There, I've typed it. So, on day two, number two ... which reminds me – there are three kinds of people in the world – those that can count, and those that can't.

Like · Comment · Promote · Share                    👍 10  💬 9

Elaine Milne, Margaret Baxter, Mark Ashpole and 7 others like this.

**Phil Evans** Go for it 😊
January 2 at 9:41pm · Unlike · 👍 1

**Mark Ashpole** Bring it on, but No lift jokes please, 😊
January 2 at 10:53pm via mobile · Like

**Phil Evans** All original and your own material please 😊
January 2 at 11:04pm · Like

**Simon Gibson** Crikey chaps - the mean streets or what? No repeats - check. Lifts - out of order. Original and own material - speak to Laura Ashley! There won't be 365 of those but I'll do as many as I can ... however, for those that want a laugh, I will also use other people's jokes 😊
January 3 at 8:09am · Like

**Simon Gibson** Dodo - extinct. Dodi - dead. Do you think Dido should be worried? (c. 1997) ...
January 3 at 7:00pm via mobile · Like

**Phil Evans** This is not easy is it 😊 Welcome to my world...... You are a brave man 😊
January 3 at 7:06pm · Unlike · 👍 1

**3 January 2013** – 4 likes – going downhill fast (see 23 January):

Footballers – not famed for their way of trying to put across how they feel without innapropriate ums and ahs, you knows and likes, over the moons and similar – like most footballers, I can't think of the word I am looking for.

Hang on, got it.

Vocabulary.

**4 January 2013** – 5 likes

... and sticking with the theme, I am extremely disgruntled, frustrated annoyed and perplexed. I have misplaced, mislaid, can't find, lost ... my Thesaurus (though strictly speaking it belongs to Roger, or Colin).

**5 January 2013** – 9 likes

Five days in and here comes effort five – as I recall how lucky we are to have a full table on Christmas Day ...

Seeing all the food out reminded me of a restaurant I went into back in the summer that serves "breakfast at any time" – I ordered French Toast, during the Renaissance ...

**6 January 2013** – 5 likes

I don't really like country music, and I don't mean to denigrate those that do. And for those that do like country music, denigrate means "put-down" ...

**7 January 2013** – 5 likes again

Dyslexics Untie !!

**8 January 2013** – a mere 3 likes for a joke I love!!

I shall be home late tonight – hoping not to find Paul Young's hat when I get in!

**9 January 2013** – 11 likes – for originality?

When I woke up this morning I thought I might do my day nine joke in German – then I thought 'no, no, no' and now my house is surrounded by the emergency services!

**10 January 2013** – 11 likes again – I could get used to this …

Recalling the wonderful summer, when I was a Games Maker someone mentioned they had heard that the next rocket sent into space by China would be full of chocolate bars - what do you think, Chinese Wispas?

Comments included: "I'm loving your daily rhetoric"; "I am really looking forward to 31 December already"; "Hey, it works for me, v. funny, thank you …" and more …
(This joke was voted the top joke at the Edinburgh Festival, in AUGUST 2013!!)

**11 January 2013** – 4 likes for my twist on an old joke

My dog's got no nose.
How does it smell?
That's a great question - normally, and I will put this in words I think you will understand, through it's amazing nose. To help you have more respect for a dog's olfactory ability, I shall compare it to a human's nose. Inside the nose of both species are bony scroll-shaped plates, known as turbinates, over which air passes. A microscopic view of this organ reveals a thick, spongy membrane that contains most of the scent detecting cells, as well as the nerves that transport information to the brain. In us humans, the area containing these odor analyzers is about one square inch, say the size of a postage stamp. If we could unfold this area in a dog, it may be as large as 60 square inches, or about the size of a piece of A4 paper.
Well, you did ask!

**12 January 2013** – 5 likes

If you have three grapefruit and a melon in one hand, and a melon and six oranges in the other hand, what have you got?

Very large hands!

**13 January 2013** – 6 likes

I have set up a group to help those with low self esteem. Starts tonight, after it gets dark, entry via the side door of the village hall (where the street light doesn't work). No need to dress up – it makes no difference to how you look ...

**14 January 2013** – 4 likes

Red sky at night, shepherds delight. Red sky in the morning, shepherds hut on fire.

**15 January 2013 – 3 likes**

**Simon Gibson**
January 15 near Burwell via mobile

What did Mick Jagger say when he discovered a Scotsman trying to steel his sheep?

'Hey, McCloud, get offa my ewe'

Like · Comment · Promote · Share     👍 3 💬 4

Then I offered my FB friends the chance to choose a topic – it was early in the year, and I should have known better – answers included (not chosen) Bankers and National Dress Up Your Pet Day, however ...

**16 January 2013** – 4 likes and seven comments, PLUS my first 'share'

When I was last away from home, I rang my wife after 2 days and after the usual felicitations asked her how the cat was. 'Dead' she says. 'Thanks very much – I am away for a week and now I have that hit me between the eyes – you could have broken the news gently' I said. She asks 'How, exactly?'
'Well, today you could have said you hadn't seen the cat for a day or so, then tomorrow say it was on the roof and wouldn't come down. The next day it had jumped into a neighbouring tree, then after a very cold night was still up there then, despite the Fire Brigade getting it down, it had died.'
'Yes, I see, how thoughtless of me' she said - 'I am sorry'.
'Anyway', I ask 'how is Uncle Jack?' 'He's on the roof' ...

**17 January 2013** – a mere 3 likes for another favourite of mine

Home late last night so I went for a curry – usually have a vindaloo but went for a tarka – it's just a little otter.

**18 January 2013** – 7 likes

It is World Day of Snowmen (really), so ...

Two snowmen talking to each other – the first one says 'can you smell carrots?' ...
(and an extra after work – so TWO jokes today) – got 7 likes for this too:
Winnie the Pooh: 'I do love fresh bacon, don't you Piglet?' 'Piglet??' ...

Also ...

... especially for the children (and my six year old son's favourite joke):

Why does Tigger smell? Well, he does play with Pooh all day!


**19 January 2013** – 7 likes again

I just saw ten hares, in a row, hopping backwards through the snow – amazing!
...
Mind you, can't say it is the first time I have seen a receding hare line ...

**20 January 2013** – 3 likes, the weather remains very bad

By jove it is cold folks – so cold that brass monkeys are lagging each other.

AND our local flasher has taken to describing himself!

**21 January 2013** – 10 likes (and the first morning I was chased for my joke of the day, because I was, quote, "late")

As if the snow weren't enough of a fag ... I was attacked by a tobacconist this morning ...
... and I've got cigars to prove it!

**22 January 2013** – 11 likes and quite a response

**Simon Gibson**
January 22 near Burwell via mobile

Sad news - my Aunty Marg has now been ill for nearly 7 weeks and the problem in her arm has spread ....

... I can't believe she's not better.

Like · Comment · Promote · Share                                    👍 11  💬 5

Mark Cross, Michelle Hoskin, William Wilson and 8 others like this.

 **Moshe Hadari** Someone should ask questions about that, in the Ausie Parliament... 🙂
January 22 at 8:59am via mobile · Like

 **Henry Saltmarsh** I have the same sentiment about your jokes.
January 22 at 9:38am · Like

 **Sue Hedger** *Groan*
January 22 at 1:23pm · Like

 **Jonny Taffs** After my wife had explained it to me, I flushed my own head down the toilet!! - keep em coming!
January 22 at 6:07pm · Unlike · 👍 1

 **Margaret Baxter** Malcolm has just read your joke! I'm scraping him off the floor! xx
January 22 at 7:17pm via mobile · Unlike · 👍 1

**23 January 2013** – 4 likes

Amazing what we don't know about our own family. Turns out my Granddad was an Olympic tobogganist.

It does explain why, since he's been ill, he has gone downhill fast.

**24 January 2013** – 4 likes

Apparently Boy George had a bit of a wild party last night – it involved five friends (all of whom ended up unconscious) and a lizard that changes colour ...
... that's right – the scene this morning is indeed:
Coma;
Coma;
Coma;
Coma;
Coma;
Chameleon.

**25 January 2013** – 8 likes, and I was to return to the "subject" later in the year ...

Does Sean Connery like herbs?
Yes ...
... but only partially.
(This may not translate well for overseas friends)

**26 January 2013** – 3 likes, topical (but apparently not that funny)
An interesting night after I set fire to the haggis:

"Fair fa' your honest, sonsie face,
Great chieftain o' the puddin-race!
Aboon them a' ye tak your place,
Painch, tripe, or thairm:
Weel are ye wordy o' a grace
As lang's my arm." ...

... that's right, I was in the Burns Unit.

**27 January 2013** – 6 likes, after a couple of days where apparently I hadn't been that visible – it appears I had changed my settings as to who could see what I was writing – some didn't complain

Next door neighbour just put up a wind turbine: big fan!

**28 January 2013** – 6 likes

We have three great children: 12, 9 and 5. My wife's idea ...
... I think they are daft names but she says we're in the digital age ...

## 29 January 2013 – 6 likes

A new title has the horse racing industry in a pickle ...
... a steamy new book for the mare in your life: that's right ...
50 Grades of Hay.

**Then, I posted this:**

**Simon Gibson**
January 29 near Newmarket

Tomorrow (all being well 30/365) is another request day - I just need a subject, please ...

Like · Comment · Promote · Share                                    💬 12

**Morwenna Clarke** Horses
January 29 at 9:23pm · Unlike · 👍 1

**Moshe Hadari** Dogs...
January 29 at 9:29pm via mobile · Unlike · 👍 2

**Elaine Milne** Broken feet.
January 29 at 9:32pm · Unlike · 👍 1

**Simon Gibson** That's one hell of a limerick folks ...
January 29 at 9:52pm · Like · 👍 2

**Martin Booth** Seahorses maybe?
January 29 at 9:54pm · Unlike · 👍 1

**Anthony Jones** The ashes ballot .....
January 29 at 9:56pm · Unlike · 👍 1

**Mark Ashpole** January......ski-ing, or new years resoloutions should cover it
January 29 at 10:00pm via mobile · Unlike · 👍 1

**Margaret Baxter** Mobile phones & conception!
January 29 at 10:07pm via mobile · Unlike · 👍 1

**Morwenna Clarke** Enough material for a month!!!!
January 29 at 10:08pm via mobile · Unlike · 👍 2

**Katy Baxter** Looking forward to at least 6 Limericks out of that lot..... 😊!! x
January 29 at 11:03pm via mobile · Unlike · 👍 1

**Simon Gibson** Thanks - here goes then ...
January 30 at 7:14am · Like

## Resulting in …
**30 January 2013** – 5 likes

An Englishman (dressed as a horse),
an Irishman (with a dog)
and a Scotsman (with a broken foot)
go into a bar …
… and the barman says …
… what is this, some kind of joke?

**31 January 2013** – 9 likes

I have been out all night with my new band, 999 Megabytes …
… we are trying to get to a gig.

## (January - delivered)

**1 February 2013** – 5 likes

My wife has taken up golf, but INSISTS on using the wrong clubs …
… she's driving a wedge between us. (FORE!)

**2 February 2013** – 4 likes

My wife has just found my lost iPod headphones – that's music to my ears.

**3 February 2013** – 9 likes

I married my wife for her looks …
… just not the ones she has been giving me lately.

**4 February 2013** – 11 likes (finding their level?)

My wife has a t-shirt with 'it is OK to look at my breasts' printed on it.
It is not the wording that bothers me …
… it's the fact that it is printed in Braille.

**5 February 2013** – 6 likes (topical)

I just received an endorsement on LinkedIn – not everyone gets one
from Chris Huhne, right?

**6 February 2013** – 8 likes

I may have mentioned my wife here before – some of you
asked me to say what she does for money ...
... it is difficult to say ...
... she sells sea shells, on the sea shore.

**7 February 2013** – 12 likes

Englishman to Irishman "why do Scuba divers always fall
backwards into the water?"
Irishman answers "because if they fell forwards they'd still be in the boat"
Not daft!

**8 February 2013** – 11 likes for the first (planned) one of the day

**Simon Gibson**
February 8, 2013 near Burwell

Went to the cemetery yesterday lunchtime to lay some flowers on a grave. As I was
standing there I noticed four grave diggers walking about with a coffin. Not unusual
I suppose.

Three hours later as I drove back past and they're still walking about with it.

I thought to myself 'they've lost the plot'.

Like · Comment · Promote · Share                                    👍11 💬1

Margaret Baxter, Ian Richardson, Greg Cummins and 8 others like this.

**Michelle Hoskin** That's made me chuckle,,,, have a great day!
February 8, 2013 at 6:23am · Unlike · 👍1

... then 3 more for a topical "gag"

100% horse meat in Findus lasagne – bet someone there has a
long face today.

**9 February 2013** – 6 likes

Sorry I am a bit late with the joke this morning, but I have been out and bought a watch!
"Analogue?"
No, just a watch ☺

**10 February 2013** – 7 likes

I went shopping yesterday afternoon. When I asked the pet shop owner for a fish he said "Do you want an aquarium?" ...
... I never knew fish had star signs!

**11 February 2013** – 6 likes

I know I am going to have a problem today – I have to go up an escalator later (and that's not a stutter), and last time it took me nearly 30 minutes to find a dog ...
... well I had to!
"Dogs must be carried on the escalator" ...

**12 February 2013** – 7 likes, and a particular favourite

Good morning! I am going through my diary, reminding myself of family birthdays, which is helped by the originality of my Grandparents when naming their children. In April there is Uncle George (23rd), before that Uncle Patrick (17th March) ...
... and TODAY – have a fantastic birthday, Uncle Pancake.

**13 February 2013** – 6 likes

Found this new cheese yesterday – not sure it will catch on, it's called 'Armageddon'. It says on the packet 'Best before END ...'

**14 February 2013** – 13 likes

Not the best start to Valentines Day. My wife: 'Does this skirt make my bum look big?'
Me: 'No! .... (so far so good) ...
.... it's the cakes you eat that make your bum look big.'

**15 February 2013** – 8 likes

When I was younger, I decided I needed to understand a bit more about  women, so I went to the library and found the perfect book – 'How to Hug' – seemed like a good (and safe) place to start ...
... only when I got home did I discover it was actually volume 12 of Encyclopedia Britannica!

**16 February 2013** – 6 likes

ID theft is no laughing matter – just ask my mate S...
(or Sid as he used to be known)

**17 February 2013** – 7 likes

The RSPCA have opened a new shop in my home town and it's really small in there ...
... there's hardly room to swing a cat!

**18 February 2013** – 12 likes

As I start a week off, I am thinking about my first job, working in a helium factory. I left on just my second day – nobody speaks to me like that!

**19 February 2013** – 5 likes

I think I have discovered why the Pope retired – his favourite feline died and left him heartbroken – so, next time someone asks you if the Pope is a cat-a-holic ...

**20 February 2013** – 6 likes – first posted from Hyderabad

I mentioned the helium factory debacle on Monday – well, my next attempt at a job was as a historian - I soon left that when I realised there was no future in it ...

**21 February 2013** – 12 likes

So, I am in Incredible !ndia –
and yesterday I got the telephone
number of the spiritual leader of Tibet –
so I called up. This morning, I received
a large white goat with a long neck –

turns out it was Dial-a-Llama ...

**22 February 2013** – 9 likes

I had planned to do a joke about sodium today, but then I thought Na ...

**23 February 2013** – 6 likes

After yesterday's joke I am in my element – apparently, the French have
sold all their gold - au revoir!

**24 February 2013** – 10 likes – back in the UK to still make a morning
delivery of joke number 55

Safe home, and I have done the decent thing and booked a table for
my wife and me tonight - what an old romantic ...
... trouble is, I am not even sure she plays snooker!!

# 25 February 2013 – 5 likes

**Simon Gibson**
February 25, 2013 near Burwell

Catching up with European news - I see the Italians have also had horse meat problems. That must be why they changed the cheese on my ready made lasagne dish - no longer is it parmesan.

Now they are using mascarpone ...

Like · Comment · Promote · Share                                     👍5 💬2

Ian Richardson, Henry Saltmarsh, Mat Fogarty and 2 others like this.

 **Lee Clarke** My great uncle Luigi started a high-speed dairy home delivery service called Mascarpone Express ...
February 25, 2013 at 7:22am · Like

 **Sharon Addison** Groan
February 25, 2013 at 8:08am · Unlike · 👍1

# 26 February 2013 – 15 likes – highest to date

For the next few days, some number jokes – statistically, six out of seven dwarves are not happy.

# 27 February 2013 – 9 likes

What do you get if you divide the circumference of a pumpkin by its diameter??
Pumpkin Pi ... (Works with cows, too)

# 28 February 2013 – 2 months in – 11 likes

Apparently ... 7/5ths of UK adults don't understand fractions ...

**1 March 2013** – 12 likes

Final one on statistics for now ..

... Apparently 1 in 5 people in the world are Chinese. There are 5 people in my family, so it must be one of them. There's me, Mum, Dad, my brother Dale Gibson and my other brother Chang – I suspect it is Dale ...

**2 March 2013** – about as risqué as they got all year – 7 likes

In recent days I have been outed for putting up 'old' jokes – well, here is one of the first jokes I ever told to get a laugh – aged 18 when Newmarket Hockey Club handed me a microphone:
I've just read a great book:
Vicious Russian Lover by Nora Bollockof

**3 March 2013** – 4 likes

My most disappointing Christmas present ever – as an excited youngster, there was the (male) doll shaped box, but when I opened it, took out what was patently NOT my desired hero, and pulled the cord, my Mum's error became all too apparent ....
... "20, 25, 30, 35 ..." That's right .... AUCTION MAN!

**4 March 2013** – 5 likes

Worrying news from the world of entertainment – Basil Brush has been diagnosed with an irregular heartbeat ... Boom, ba, ba, ba, boom, ba, boom

**5 March 2013** – 5 likes

What has four legs and a tail and says boo? A cow with a cold.

**6 March 2013** – 12 likes

Two fish swim into a concrete wall. One turns to the other and says 'Dam!'

# 7 March 2013 – my birthday!! – 9 likes

 **Simon Gibson**
March 7, 2013 near Cambridge

What has wings, a long tail and wears a bow?

A birthday pheasant.

Like · Comment · Promote · Share 👍9 💬5

Ian Richardson, Ravi Kumar, Janet Hawson and 6 others like this.

 **Sam Lovelace-Walne** And may you day be filled with such pheasants - happy birthday x
March 7, 2013 at 7:45am · Unlike · 👍1

 **Mat Fogarty** happy Birthday simon hope you have a great day
March 7, 2013 at 9:53am · Unlike · 👍1

 **Henry Saltmarsh** HAPPY BIRTHDAY SIMON. 🙂
March 7, 2013 at 11:03am · Unlike · 👍1

 **Aurora Tancock** Happy Birthday Simon!
March 7, 2013 at 1:34pm · Unlike · 👍1

 **Brad Myers** Happy Birthday!
March 7, 2013 at 8:47pm · Unlike · 👍1

# 8 March 2013 – 7 likes

Yesterday I took a call on the mobile – one of those phishing ones ...
I decided to play along:

Hello Sir, is that Simon Gibson?
Yes.
Can I check a couple of details please?
Oh, OK ....
When is your birthday?
7th March.
Really, it is your birthday today?
Yes.
Which year?
Every year

**9 March 2013** – 10 likes

Two parrots sat on a perch.
One turns to the other and says ...

... "Can you smell fish?"

**10 March 2013** – 12 likes

Two fish in a tank. One says to the other ...
... 'Do you know how to drive this thing?'

**11 March 2013** – 12 likes

A bear walks into a bar. He says to the barman,
"Please may I have a pint of beer and
... um, ... er, ... a packet of crisps"

The barman says ... "What's with the big pause?"
(Regular readers please note, the bear could a) talk and b) was polite)

**12 March 2013** – 9 likes

Two snakes, slithering along. One says to the other 'Are we poisonous?'
'I don't know, why do you ask!' says the second snake.
'Oh, I just bit my tongue.'

**13 March 2013** – 2 likes (losing my touch ...) and I love this joke

I went to a dyslexic rave last night – amidst the banging tunes and
flashing lights I found a fellow in the corner of the barn trying to inject
himself with a heron.

**14 March 2013** – 9 likes

Apparently, in his formative years, Pope Francis was agnostic, an
insomniac and dyslexic ...
... oh the nights he lay awake at night wondering if there was a dog.

**15 March 2013** – Red Nose Day – 5 likes

(Last of the (current) dyslexia trilogy)
Did you hear about the dyslexic Iranian radical?
... He spent 20 years trying to assassinate Willie Rushton.

**16 March 2013** – 11 likes

The police arrested two children in our street last night, one was drinking battery acid, the other was eating fireworks ...
... they charged one and let the other off.

**17 March 2013** – 12 likes (Milton Jones, this one)

I was at the cashpoint yesterday when an elderly lady came to the machine next to me and asked if I would help her check her balance ...
... so I did ... and I pushed her over.

**18 March 2013** – 4 likes

Me: Dr, I am worried about my brother – he thinks he is a chicken.
Dr: Why don't you take him to the hospital. They'll keep him in and do some tests.
Me: Can't do that – we need the eggs!

**19 March 2013** – 14 likes

News just in.
Apparently Paul McCartney was more generous in his divorce agreement than we first thought.
He bought Heather a plane.
(And a Phillips Ladyshave for the other leg).

**20 March 2013** – 14 likes

So, you think you are fit?
MY GRANDAD started walking 5 miles a day when he was 76.
He is now 87 ...
... and we have no idea where he is!

**21 March 2013** – 10 likes – just a bit of fun

We had some weird weather here yesterday, so I switched on the Weather Channel, and they give forecasts for everywhere!

Hold on to your hats folks.
Apparently, in Iraq today, it will be Sunni in places and Shiite in others ...

**22 March 2013** – 17 likes – new record!

More strange happenings.

The last two nights, someone has broken in to our back garden and added about an inch of compost to where I grow my vegetables.
I have no idea who it could be, the police are baffled, no one was seen ...
... the plot thickens.

**23 March 2013** – 7 likes

Odd behaviour from a child at our school – they bring in two bags, EVERY day – beginning to think they might be bi-satchel.

**24 March 2013** – 11 likes

Isn't life funny – I was just recalling an old girlfriend the other day, from Holland. She was nice, but odd, with inflatable footwear ...
... then yesterday I hear she's popped her clogs.

**25 March 2013** – 10 likes

I am really getting into e-books or, as anyone reading this from Yorkshire knows them, books.

**26 March 2013** – 12 likes

Say what you like about the deaf ...

**27 March 2013** – 2 today – first, the planned one, then one responding to the news – 13 likes

I know we all work hard, but I have been getting really tired and looking for something to do on my days off have decided to give meditation a go. Well, it beats sitting round doing nothing ...

Then ... with 6 likes:

No more Border Agency – what will we do for sheepdogs?

**28 March** 2013 – 12 likes

Writing about meditation yesterday reminded me of that oft-quoted Gandhi. What many don't know is that eating as he did gave him really bad breath (which he couldn't get rid of), he was (as you may recall) incredibly thin and as he didn't wear shoes his feet got really terrible hard skin. That's right, he was ...
... a super calloused fragile mystic, hexed by halitosis (tip – best read quickly).

**29 March 2013** – 13 likes

I found myself in a lovely part of southern Ireland, but very slightly lost, needing to get to Dublin. So, seeing a likely fellow walking towards me, I politely asked him the quickest way. "Are you walking or driving" he says. I reply "Driving".
His helpful response: "That's the quickest way" ...

**30 March 2013** – 6 likes

Fed up of all the talk about war in Korea? Well, for the next three days, assuming the world doesn't end, three career jokes ...

The job I was most surprised to be fired from was as a psychic – I didn't see that coming!

**31 March 2013** – 7 likes

Next I went for an interview as a bug sorter – I have reason to believe it went well. I boxed all the right ticks.

**1 April 2013** – 8 likes

Things didn't work for me at the specialist spice company – I couldn't cut the mustard.

## 2 April 2013 – 12 likes

So there I am, in a smart restaurant, and I fancy some squid. They keep them in a tank and take them out for cooking – killing – only when ordered.

I order.

Sorry Sir, says the waiter, you can't have the squid. I ask why not and he explains.

Having taken my order he goes into the kitchen and tells the chef, Gervais, of my order. The problem is the squid, getting on a bit, and beginning to look a bit hairy round the mouth, has become a favourite in the kitchen, and Gervais cannot bring himself to kill it. The waiter then asks everyone else in the kitchen, explains that a valued customer (me) will be disappointed if the squid isn't served.

Even Hans, the extremely butch German in charge of cleaning the cutlery and dishes, even HE cannot bring himself to deliver the blow to the slightly pistachio coloured 'friend' of the kitchen staff.
The waiter finishes this explanation and I realise the problem – it appears that what I learnt as a child is still true today ...

Hans that do dishes are soft as Gervais, with mild green hairy lipped squid.

## 3 April 2013 – 3 likes

Ronseal does indeed do exactly what it says on the tin.
Ask my younger brother. He bought a tin of hard wearing varnish, which ... causes nausea, dizziness and headaches if ingested!

## 4 April 2013 – 9 likes

My Mum and Dad's first names are Pearl and Dean.

I call them Mama and Papa papaa papaa papaa pa pa pa, papaa papaa pa paaaaaa ...

**5 April 2013** – 8 likes

To the bloke on crutches, wearing top to toe camouflage, who knicked my wallet – look out, mate ...

... you can hide, but you can't run!

**6 April 2013** – new tax year and 5 likes

Today starts a short series of stuff that doesn't make sense ...

Why did Kamikaze pilots wear helmets?

**7 April 2013** – 10 likes

And another thing ...

Where is the next generation of seedless grapes coming from?

**8 April 2013** – 12 likes

And another thing ...

What did the bloke who invented the drawing board go back to?

**9 April 2013** – 4 likes, despite this being a personal favourite ...

And another thing ...

If music is the food of love, why can't rabbits play banjos?

**10 April 2013** – 11 likes

Got woken up last night when the dog next door blew up it's kennel – bloody Yorkshire Terrorist!

**11 April 2013** – 9 likes

My wife loves her piano more than me – can you tell? She left me this note yesterday:

'Gone Chopin (with Liszt); Bach in a minuet.' – with Stevie Ray Plewes.

**12 April 2013** – 6 likes

The children are learning about jobs at school. Wendy says her Dad is a Professor. George says his Mum is a Dr.

Johnny (they are always called Johnny) says his Dad plays the piano in a brothel.

Appalled, the teacher, not believing him, calls Dad that night. "No, of course I don't play the piano on a brothel" he tells her. "I am a lawyer – how do I explain that to a seven year old?" — with Stevie Ray Plewes.

**13 April 2013** – 12 likes

2 aerials met on a roof, fell in love and got married – the ceremony was rubbish, but the reception ...

**14 April 2013** – 9 likes

Went to see a therapist – he told me I have a problem with vengeance – we'll see about that!

**15 April 2013** – 10 likes

After many years, two Eskimos eventually got the kayak of their dreams. Out on the lake one day, they found they were getting cold, so they lit a fire in the bottom of it ... and it sank.

This proves beyond doubt that you cannot have your kayak and heat it.

**16 April 2013** – 7 likes

Was in the pub last night when a fellow I vaguely know asked if I would like a game of darts. I said I would. 'Nearest the bull goes first'. I said.

'Baa' he said.

I said 'Moo'.

'You're closest' he replied.

## 17 April 2013 – 9 likes

My friend is a hunt saboteur and I am not sure he is cut out for it. Today is the day of the big local hunt, and I asked him what he had planned.
'I've already done it' he told me 'I shall stay at home'.
'What have you done then?' I asked.
'I went out last night ... ' he replied. '... and I shot the fox'.

## 18 April 2013 – 13 likes

I used to share a flat with a friend, and to say he wasn't the sharpest tool in the box ...
Found him in the kitchen one morning, fridge door open, staring at the top shelf. He was still there 20 minutes later ...
... which was when I realised that the orange juice carton had 'Concentrate' written on it.

## 19 April 2013 – 11 likes and comments

**Simon Gibson**
April 19, 2013 near Burwell

I just read about an Indian mystic who had all his wisdom teeth extracted without anaesthetic ...

... apparently ...

... he wanted to transcend dental medication.

(I guess it was done at 2:30)

Like · Comment · Promote · Share                 👍11 💬8

Henry Saltmarsh, Morwenna Clarke, Ian Richardson and 8 others like this.

**Mark Hanna** Aargh! Lol
April 19, 2013 at 6:39am · Unlike · 👍1

**Elaine Milne** Hmmmm......
April 19, 2013 at 6:49am · Like

**Anthony Jones** Better than yesterday's. at least I understand this one !!! Lol
April 19, 2013 at 7:20am · Unlike · 👍1

**20 April 2013** – 6 likes

So, having discovered a new mark on her face, and finding it was somewhat irritating, she went to see the Dr.

Looking very carefully at the area, under a strong magnifying glass, the Dr says "This is remarkable – on your face you have a tiny pond, I can see a bench, an oak tree, some ducks, flowers and, no, wait, this can't be right – children playing!"

"Oh dear" she says – "what does this mean?"

"It's OK" says the Dr – "it is just a beauty spot".

**21 April 2013** – 10 likes

Last night, a bloke in the pub offered me eight legs of venison for fifty quid.

What do you reckon, too dear?

**22 April 2013** – 8 likes

What bites and talks in code?
A morse-quito ...
... and you thought it was going to be a Luis Saurez joke!

**23 April 2013** – 14 likes

I got stung by bees at the weekend – £10 for a jar of honey!

**24 April 2013** – 7 likes

What has three heads, two tails, eight legs, a beak, two noses, six eyes and one pair of arms?

A man riding a horse with a chicken on his head.

**25 April 2013** – 7 likes

Haven't seen my brother for a bit and when we met up he said he thought I had put on some weight. Now he's not the sharpest tool in the box, but I wasn't expecting what happened next.

'Get us a Fonda video then' I suggested, 'if you think I should be getting fitter – and we can watch it together. That should help.'

Anyone want to borrow 'On Golden Pond'?

**26 April 2013** – 17 likes

When I was a lad I so wanted a bicycle. I used to pray for one every night.

Then, when I was about 12, I realised God doesn't work like that.

So I stole one and prayed for forgiveness.

**27 April 2013** – got 6 likes – very close to one in August ... (10.8.13)

Two jump leads walk into a bar, and the barman says 'don't start anything'

**28 April 2013** – got 14 likes

My first girlfriend was gorgeous, one of twins. She was tall and blonde with a winning smile.

Friends used to rib me about whether I ever took the wrong one out. I am pretty sure I didn't.

Her brother had a beard!

**29 April 2013** – 1 – got 4 likes

On the subject of girlfriends, I did once go out with an agoraphobic girl, who wasn't the brightest creature. I was a bit naughty though – I told her she was stupid (not a nice thing to do). Her reply?

'You're no rocket surgeon yourself.'

At least I know she's not out to get me ...

**29 April 2013** – 2 – got 2 likes

Don't buy anyone from the North East 'The Joy of Six' in the next few days – it may not get the reaction you hoped for!!

**30 April 2013** – 10 likes

So there I am in the Chinese restaurant, and after I have seen the head waiter, a duck waddles over to me.

"Hello Sir, you are looking good tonight" it says. "I like what you are wearing and that aftershave is very alluring." The duck then proceeds to give me a rose, and waddles off.

Incensed, I call over the head waiter. "Is everything alright Sir" he enquires?

"Not really" I reply. "This duck came over, said some nice stuff about me and then gave me a rose."

"Yes Sir" says the waiter "and the problem is?"

"I ordered A romatic Duck" ...

Fisher

**1 May 2013** – 10 likes

Many years ago I was lucky enough to have dinner with Garry Kasparov. I remember it clearly – wonderful food, a rose in a vase, on a check tablecloth, attentive staff – a real privilege.

The only problem was, it took him 2 hours to pass the salt!

**2 May 2013** – 18 likes

I get a call – "The car won't start" says my wife "I think there is water in the carburettor".

"Honestly, how would, you know? You don't even know what the carburettor is" I reply.

"I am telling you, there is water in the carburettor, I know there is" she insists.

"Well, let me be the judge of that" I reply – "Where is the car?"

"In the swimming pool".

**3 May 2013** – 12 likes

As I walked through the shopping area, a very attractive young lady was walking towards me wearing a very well filled T-shirt with the word "Guess" on it.

I said "Implants" but apparently it is a brand name, not a request ...

**4 May 2013** – 10 likes and comments

 **Simon Gibson**
May 4, 2013

Luke here, just because it is May The Fourth, it doesn't mean I am going to Leia Star Wars joke on you. If you were Darth enough to think that, Yoda be wrong.

(This written with the assistance of a Sith (sorry, six) year old! It's Obi-Wan day, get over it ...) — with David Batchelor.

Like · Comment · Promote · Share          👍 10 💬 7

Margaret Baxter, Dean Hobbs, Anthony Jones and 7 others like this.

 **Moshe Hadari** My, The Farce Bee' With You...
May 4, 2013 at 8:16am · Unlike · 👍 1

 **Moshe Hadari** And, LOOK ... I KNOW what you are getting for Christmas !!! Yes , really. Because...... (wait for it...) (through a respirator...) "I felt your PRESENTS..."
May 4, 2013 at 8:20am · Unlike · 👍 1

 **Simon Gibson** There goes my Christmas Eve joke ...
May 4, 2013 at 8:41am · Like

 **Anthony Jones** Love it
May 4, 2013 at 8:58am · Unlike · 👍 1

 **Anthony Jones** You've been holding that one since jan 1 st I'm sure !!!
May 4, 2013 at 8:58am · Unlike · 👍 1

 **Simon Gibson** It was written at the kitchen table three weeks ago - real team effort!!
May 4, 2013 at 9:48am · Like

 **Dean Hobbs** Very good 🙂
May 4, 2013 at 10:46am · Unlike · 👍 1

**5 May 2013** – 11 likes

My Grandad had some great sayings – one of his favourites was 'fight fire with fire' – probably accounts for why they threw him out of the Fire Brigade.

## 6 May 2013 – 16 likes

I was out at a wedding reception last night, appropriately togged out in my finest morning suit, and by the end of it I really felt like Fred Astaire. This was not because I was dancing the night away though.

As the waiter brought my dessert of treacle sponge and cream, he tripped and threw it all over me.

Pudding on my top hat, pudding on my white tie, pudding on my tails.

## 7 May 2013 – 14 likes

The young man in a cafe is ready with his order – a gorgeous young waitress comes over and asks for his order – 'I'd like a quickie, please' he says, and for his trouble she slaps him and runs off, clearly upset. Another waitress comes across, slightly older, perhaps sent because she is more experienced? 'Can I help you Sir?' she asks ... 'Yes, he says, I'd still like a quickie' – and she slaps him and walks away.

Somewhat shocked, the young man slouches back in the chair, and the elderly lady sat on the next table leans over and says, quietly but firmly ...

'Young man, I think you'll find it is pronounced 'quiche' ...'

## 8 May 2013 – 14 likes

So, two brothers (not sure of their nationality), let's call them Mick and Paddy, each decide to buy a pig. They get them home and put them in the back yard. As they look out of their kitchen window that evening, Paddy says to Mick 'Mick, we haven't thought about this – how are we going to know which is which?'

Mick suggests that they cut an ear of Paddy's pig, and that way they will know which is which. 'Great idea' says Paddy, and that's what they do. When they wake up the next morning, Mick shouts out to Paddy – 'Your pig has only gone and eaten the ear off my pig – now what do we do – they both only have one ear now'.

Paddy suggests they cut the ear off his pig again, leaving him with the no-ear pig – 'Surely it won't eat the second ear off your pig?' – they agree, and for a couple of days, all is well – Paddy has the pig with no ears and Mick has the one-eared pig. Then, tragedy strikes ... and once again, Mick finds that Paddy's pig has eaten the remaining ear off his, and they both have no-eared pigs.

Getting somewhat exasperated, as this was Mick's idea in the first place, Paddy says 'What do we do now to tell them apart?' Mick suggests they cut the tail off his pig, as a) it's been his pig doing the chewing and b) it seems unlikely that any pig would want to eat that!

The very next day, when they look out of the window, there are the two pigs, both with no ears and no tails. Paddy is incandescent with rage, and shouts at Mick 'What do we do now to be able to tell which is which??'

Mick replies 'Well, maybe you should have the brown pig and I'll have the pink pig?'

## 9 May 2013 – 8 likes

You may recall I introduced you to Paddy and Mick yesterday. Well, Paddy famously likes a drink, and has developed one that sorts out part of that terrible morning after hangover, regardless of how much he drinks the night before ...

... he now drinks just white wine and windolene - he still feels rough in the morning, but his eyes are bright and clear.

**10 May 2013** – 7 likes and 1 share

Our new friends Paddy and Mick are at work in the local public park. Paddy is diligently digging a hole, carefully placing the spent soil to one side in a pile. Mick then gets that soil and equally carefully puts it back in the hole, filling it up.

The man on the bench watches this with incredulity – after he has seen them do it a third time, he approaches and asks what they are doing.

'Well' says Paddy, 'usually there are three of us. I dig the hole, Sean plants the tree, and Mick fills it back in.'

'Sean rang in sick today, but that doesn't mean Mick and I should stop work for the day, does it?'

**11 May 2013** – 7 likes

Today is 131/365, and I reference joke 2/365 ... keep up:

When it comes to binary numbers, there are only 10 types of people in the world – those that understand them and those that don't.

**12 May 2013** – 12 likes

After several more 'in depth' jokes, a few days dedicated to the younger followers of this year long challenge (and before you say it, I know it is as much a challenge for you lot as it is for me) ... so

Q. What is hairy and flys?
A. A hot-air baboon.

**13 May 2013** – 10 likes

Q. What do you get when you cross a cat with a parrot?
A. A carrot.

(For Josh, — with Bazza Haynes and Joy Haynes.

**14 May 2013** – 9 likes

Q. What do you get if you cross a cocker spaniel, a poodle and a cockerel?

A. A cockapoodledoo.

(That went a lot better than it might have done ...)

**15 May 2013** – 11 likes

Me: Doctor, Doctor, I have got a sore throat.

Doctor: Go over to the window and stick your tongue out.

Me: Will that help?

Doctor: No, I just don't like my neighbours ...

**16 May 2013** – 5 likes

Q. How many ears did Davy Crockett have?

A. Three. A left ear, a right ear, and a wild frontier.

**17 May 2013** – 6 likes

I sense some of you are tiring of the Q & A idea, so let's crank it up a bit for Friday ... though this joke is sanitised! You might want to make a drink too, it's a bit longer than recent offerings ...

So, the man who survived eight weeks on a desert island is being interviewed. He explains that though initially convinced he would be rescued, he quickly realised he had to fend for himself.

'What did you do for water?' he is asked – he goes on to say how once he had worked out that drinking rain from leaves and coconut 'milk' was OK, he learnt how to make a fire and would boil sea water in the coconut shells – very resourceful. 'And for food ...?'

'I would eat whatever looked like it wouldn't kill me – and in the end I waded out into the water and would catch a fish with my bare hands.' 'Wow', says the interviewer – 'was there anything else we take for granted that you learnt to cope with in your new situation for all that time?' 'Well of course, I am a red-blooded man, and I missed the company of a woman' he says. 'However, I did have one experience' he goes on ...

'I was getting a bit 'desperate', and on the beach one day I spotted an ostrich on the beach, it's head down, and it's shapely bottom called to me' (as I say, sanitised).
Incredulous, the interviewer gasps – 'you are not going to tell me you had sex with an ostrich??' 'I did' the man says.
'May I ask, what was that like?' whispers the interviewer ...
'Well', says the ship-wrecked man, 'it was alright for the first 100 yards, while we were in step ...'

**18 May 2013** – 13 likes

After yesterday's change of pace, I had a huge reaction (ooo errr) and several requests NOT to do any joke today involving rude words, religion, royalty, stereotypes, disability, homophobia, drugs or gambling!

Unfortunately, that ruins my best joke, the punch line to which is:

'Bloody hell Archbishop' said the Queen, 'how about that daft Irish one legged lesbian crackhead winning the lottery again!'

Oh well ...

**19 May 2013** – 15 likes and comments and 1 share

The baby is being baptised, and the vicar is chatting to the parents beforehand. 'Baptism is a serious business, are you prepared for it?' 'We think so' says the father – 'my wife has made some appetisers and cut some very neat cucumber sandwiches, plus made some scones ...' 'That's not really what I meant – how about spiritually?' says the vicar. 'Oh yes, of course' says the father. 'We've got that covered – I went out and bought gin, whisky AND vodka ...'

**20 May 2013** – 5 likes

And remaining on the religious 'theme' ...
Q. What did the Buddhist Monk say to the hot dog seller?
A. Make me one with everything ...

**21 May 2013** – 5 likes

The definition of an optimist? An accordion player with an agent.

**22 May 2013** – 19 likes

It is 3am, and the door bell rings. Vaguely awake, the husband nudges his wife to go and see who it is - "It is 3am" she says, "you go". Stumbling from his bed, the husband opens the window a touch and looks down, but it is pitch black outside, and the park opposite is quiet, as is the road. Then he hears it ...
"Give us a push mate" – realising that he may have been spotted, he quietly gets back into bed, hoping they will go away.
No more than 30 seconds later, the husband hears a knock at the door "Please, give us a push mate – I'd really appreciate it." His wife hears it too. "Go on, do the charitable things for him" she says "it is 3am, and you wouldn't want to be out and about on a night like this without someone offering to help, would you?"
"I suppose not", says the nevertheless disgruntled husband. "I am coming down" he shouts from the window. Slippers and dressing gown on, he goes downstairs, unlocks the door and opens it to find no-one there. Stepping a couple of yards outside, he looks left and right and still can't see anyone.
"Hey, you that needs the push, where are you?"
"Over here" comes a voice "in the park, on the swings" ...

**23 May 2013** – 4 likes

How do you know when you run out of invisible ink?

**24 May 2013** – 12 likes

It's Friday, so, especially for Jonny Taffs, here we go:

I like to go and help at the local Nursing Home, and the other day I was there for lunchtime. Old Fred, slightly deaf, a bit short of memory but a great fellow, asked me to sit with him. I of course agreed.

As we sat, a really rather attractive young girl came over – it turns out she is the waitress, there to earn some money between terms at University. She leans in to Fred, her low cut top .... anyway, you get the picture. Then, in a rather husky (and slightly too loud) voice, she says in his ear "would you like supersex?"
I can hardly control myself but Fred is the personification of calm as he thinks, then turns his head, looks her in the eye and says ...

"What sort of soup?"

**25 May 2013** – 15 likes

Mum rang me last night – she hasn't seen the grandchildren for a while, and it's her fault – you see, we have a dog, and she is rather wary of him, so she won't come round – I decided to try again.

"Mum, great to hear from you. Would you like to come to lunch on Sunday and see the family?"

"You know I would" she says "but that dog worries me" ...

"It's OK Mum" I reassure her. "I've had him castrated."

There is a pause, and then she says ...

"Actually, I've been worried about him biting me!"

**26 May 2013** – 5 likes

What happens if you get scared half to death – TWICE?

**27 May 2013** – 10 likes

UNLIKE my amazing friend Anthony Jones, my sister has been putting on weight recently, and on Saturday she caused a man to break his arm! She was in the High Street when she received a text message – this poor fellow jumped out of the way and fell heavily trying to avoid her – he thought she was reversing ...

**28 May 2013** – 12 likes

So George Michael has had another accident, poor love. This time though, it seems it's not entirely his fault ...

Apparently, some fellow swerved in front of him on a scooter.

Even the police report exonerates George, blaming a ....

.... careless Vespa.

**29 May 2013** – 10 likes

I have an inferiority complex – I'm not a medical man, but I bet it's a bad one.

(Saving one for tomorrow which, for regulars, won't have come quickly enough – tomorrow is day 150/365!!)

**30 May 2013** – 14 likes and 1 share!

Apple have been thrilled with the initial responses to their latest product. It is called the iBreast, and is a 70gb chip that stores music, and which can be implanted to a woman's breast so that she can have her music with her wherever she goes.

Apple executives were initially worried that women may think it sexist, but the reaction of women's groups in the UK and US has been fantastic – one spokesperson (!) being quoted as saying:

"We love it! For too many years, men have been looking at women's breasts and not listening to them".

(150/365)

**31 May 2013** – 8 likes

(The star of this joke could be from Aylesbury, Cardiff, Wexford, anywhere really - adjust before telling for maximum effect ...)
He comes home drunk, with a duck under his arm.
 'You've been drinking again' says his wife, 'and what's with the duck?'
 'I won it in a competition at the pub. It was 'who has the longest todger' and I won, I won the duck.'
 'They lined up all the men in the pub and then measured us'.
 Now a little prouder than angry, his wife nevertheless looks a bit peeved, and chastises him – 'you didn't show everyone in the pub all of what's meant to be kept between me and you did you?'

 'Of course not' he says – 'I just showed them enough to win the duck' ...

**1 June 2013** – 13 likes

**Simon Gibson**
June 1

Especially for Bazza Haynes on your birthday 😊

Guess who I bumped into at the opticians the other day?

Everyone!!

Like · Comment · Promote · Share                    👍 13  💬 1

**2 June 2013** – 10 likes

**Simon Gibson**
June 2 near Burwell

This year marks the 90th anniversary of the death of Sir James Dewar, who invented the thermos flask - he's been dead a while, but is rumoured to be still warm ...

Like · Comment · Promote · Share                    👍 10  💬 1

**3 June 2013** – 11 likes

I had my hair cut on Saturday. I take my hat off to my barber – well, it seems only fair, to give him a chance ...

**4 June 2013** – 9 likes

So, still on the subject of hair, many years ago (natch), I was up in Newcastle and visited a local barber. 'What can I do for you?' he asked. 'I'd like a perm' was my response ...

'OK' he clears his throat ...'I wandered lonely as a cloud ...' (Translations available into American English, etc.)

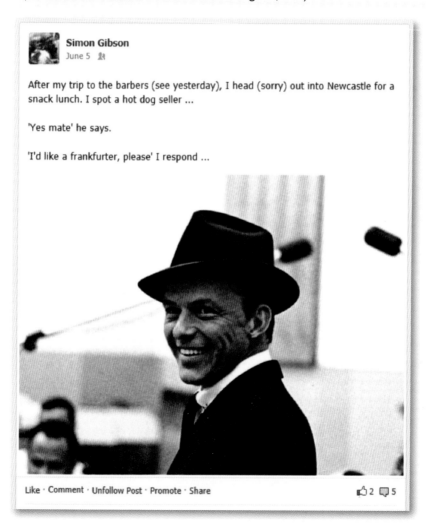

**Simon Gibson**
June 5

After my trip to the barbers (see yesterday), I head (sorry) out into Newcastle for a snack lunch. I spot a hot dog seller ...

'Yes mate' he says.

'I'd like a frankfurter, please' I respond ...

Like · Comment · Unfollow Post · Promote · Share          👍2 💬5

Two drinking friends, who are airplane mechanics, are in the hangar at London Heathrow airport; it is foggy and they have nothing to do.

One of them says to the other, "Jim, have you got anything to drink?"

Jim says, "I am afraid not, but I hear you can drink jet fuel, and that it will give you a real buzz."

So they drink it, get drunk and have a great time.

The following morning, Jim gets up and is surprised he feels good, in fact, he feels great – no hangover! The phone rings, it is his friend, Mike.

Mike says "Jim, how do you feel?"

Jim says "I feel great!"

"I feel great too! You don't have a hangover?" says Mike.

"No - that jet fuel is great stuff – no hangover – we ought to do this more often."

"Well, we could, but there's just one thing."

"What's that?" says Jim ...

"Well, that's what I called to tell you. For goodness sake don't fart, I'm calling you from the Seychelles."

**7 June 2013** – 8 likes

**Simon Gibson**
June 7

So the flight went well, and there was great news for me - on the entertainment package with BA there was one of my favourite films, Groundhog Day, with one of my favourite actors, Bill Murray.

I could watch that film again and again ...

(especially for Margaret Baxter, sorry your daily 'fix' is late ... though it is early here)

Like · Comment · Promote · Share          👍 8   💬 3

Mark Ashpole, John F Nichols, Dean Hobbs and 5 others like this.

**Margaret Baxter** Thanks Simon, bless you! I'll try and be patient! You have a great time xx
June 7 at 1:52pm via mobile · Unlike · 👍 1

**Elaine Milne** I got it today! 😊 x
June 7 at 2:37pm via mobile · Unlike · 👍 1

**Mat Fogarty** Simon my favorite joke of yours maybe we could have it again or maybe at you presentation have a great meeting
June 8 at 4:57am via mobile · Unlike · 👍 1

Write a comment...

## 8 June 2013 – 5 likes

**Simon Gibson**
June 8 near Philadelphia, PA, United States

For my friend Mat Fogarty ... 'twas always planned.

So the flight went well, and there was great news for me - on the entertainment package with BA there was one of my favourite films, Groundhog Day, with one of my favourite actors, Bill Murray.

I could watch that film again and again and again ...

Like · Comment · Promote · Share          👍 5 💬 3

Lloyd Hardwick, Moshe Hadari, Anthony Jones and 2 others like this.

**Anthony Jones** Brilliant. U groundhog !!
June 8 at 1:21pm via mobile · Like

**Katy Baxter** Hehehe!!
June 8 at 1:24pm via mobile · Unlike · 👍 1

**Mat Fogarty** Thanks brilliant absolutely brilliant
June 8 at 2:59pm via mobile · Unlike · 👍 1

Write a comment...

## 9 June 2013 – 7 likes

So, the flight went well ... no, I wouldn't do that to you.

My New Years resolution for 2013? To stop putting things off ...

## 10 June 2013 – 10 likes

I have been thinking about this joke for sometime ...

Procrastination: working tomorrow for a better today

**Simon Gibson**
June 11

When I was younger I came up with a brilliant business plan - to build bungalows for dwarfs - there was just one tiny flaw ...

Like · Comment · Promote · Share     👍 15  💬 10

Mark Ashpole, Ian Richardson, Ash Chauhan and 12 others like this.

**Sam Lovelace-Walne** It took a moment!
June 11 at 12:37pm via mobile · Unlike · 👍 1

**Dean Hobbs** Excellent! 🙂
June 11 at 12:57pm via mobile · Unlike · 👍 1

**Michelle Hoskin** Just for us....
June 11 at 12:58pm via mobile · Unlike · 👍 1

**Lee Clarke** It's the way you tell them.... 🙂
June 11 at 4:35pm via mobile · Unlike · 👍 1

**Mark Ashpole** Your jokes have just moved to another level , thank you. M
June 12 at 5:39am via mobile · Unlike · 👍 2

**David Wright** this is typical of your low humour
June 12 at 7:13am · Unlike · 👍 1

**Lee Clarke** I was floored by that one...
June 12 at 7:32am via mobile · Unlike · 👍 1

**David Wright** i hope all the dwarves take a break from putting turn ups on their underpants to protest this sort of humour !!
June 12 at 10:29am · Like

**Simon Gibson** I have already had complaints David - six out of seven are not happy!
June 12 at 10:40am · Like · 👍 1

**12 June 2013** – 16 likes

It was UK and Irish night here last night – which essentially means Irish night! It reminded me of my friend Mick ...
Mick is an Irishman, and he and his wife discovered that their next door neighbour had bought a dog when, on the first day, in the garden next door, all it did was bark. Woof, woof, woof, woof and woof all day. The same the next day – all it did was bark – woof, woof, woof, woof, woof. Imagine then how they felt when after a second night of little sleep, they woke on day three to hear this, from the garden next door:
Woof, woof, woof, woof, woof.

"We can't continue with that coming from next door" says Mick's wife.

"Right" says Mick "I shall do something about it" and he heads out of their house to go next door. The barking stops for a couple of minutes, then starts again just as Mick comes back into the house, only it seems louder.
Woof, woof, woof, woof, woof.

"What have you done?" asks his wife.

"I have put the dog in our garden to see how THEY like it!"

**13 June 2013** – 10 likes

Time flies like an arrow;

Fruit flies like a banana!

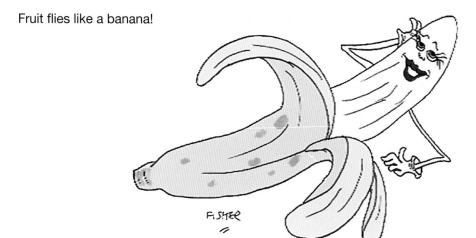

F. SHEE

**14 June 2013** – 16 likes

Me: Doctor, I have just returned from America, and I keep thinking I am either  Mickey Mouse, Donald Duck or Pluto.

Doctor: How long have you been having these Disney spells??

**15 June 2013** – 14 likes

News from the Queen's Birthday Honours List – the man who invented the zip fastener gets a lifetime peerage, henceforth to be known as ...

Lord of the Flies.

**16 June 2013** – 11 likes

With all the wet weather, I recall a trip to Scotland – having spent two weeks in a nice hotel in a village where it rained for the whole time, I was out on the last day, umbrella, wellies, etc., when I saw a little lad in the street.

'Does the weather ever change here?' I asked him.

'I don't know' he replied, 'I am only six' ...

**17 June 2013** – 9 likes

I have joined a reggae band as their triangle player –
I just stand there and ting ...

**18 June 2013** – 14 likes

A dyslexic walks into a bra ...

**19 June 2013** – 7 likes

I do enjoy trying to pack myself into a small suitcase. I can hardly contain myself ...

**20 June 2013** – 16 likes

I manage money for a part-time teacher who also does some work as a fortune teller - we agreed on short-term medium risk.

**21 June 2013** – 7 likes

Sticking with the financial theme:

If you laid all the economists in the world end to end ...

... they still wouldn't reach a conclusion.

**22 June 2013** – 22 likes

**Simon Gibson**
June 22

Too expensive to have your shirt dry cleaned? Just donate it to the local charity shop - they'll clean it and hang it up. Next day you can buy it back for £1 - everyone wins!!

Like · Comment · Promote · Share          👍 22  💬 2

Ronnie Muhl, Anthony Morris, Aurora Tancock and 19 others like this.

**Moshe Hadari** Fab financial planning advice... 😊
June 22 at 10:13am via mobile · Unlike · 👍 1

**Anthony Jones** Bloody brilliant idea !!!! Lol
June 22 at 10:16am via mobile · Unlike · 👍 1

Write a comment...

**23 June 2013** – 11 likes

I am very excited. I have come to an important decision.
Next week I am going to set the bar really high ...
... because I am a rubbish limbo dancer.

**24 June 2013** – 8 likes and loads of comments

FACT: we had a nasty accident yesterday involving our car and a deer – quite a shock and though people all OK, car not. We were very, very lucky to all walk away unscathed.

So ... here it comes folks ...

Q. What do you call a deer with no eyes?
A. No idea.

**25 June 2013** – 8 likes

Q. What do you call a deer with no eyes and no legs?
A. Still no idea.
(Look out for the third (and therefore final) part of the 'Deer Trilogy' tomorrow ...)

**26 June 2013** – 14 likes

What do you get if you cross Bambi with a ghost?

(wait for it, wait for it ...)

A. bamBOO!

**27 June 2013** – 20 likes

Sean Connery gets a call from his agent. 'Sean, I have a new job for you – it pays really well, and you need to be there on good time. 10-ish.'

Sean replies, 'Ten-ish? Will I need to take my own racket?'

**Simon Gibson**
June 28

OK, fantastic reaction yesterday, so I'll go for one more ... thanks everyone, nearly halfway (179/365) and I have some exciting ideas for when we get into the final stretch ...

People say Sean Connery found his niche.

She was playing hide and seek with his nephew all the time ...

Like · Comment · Promote · Share          👍 15  💬 9

Morwenna Clarke, Mark Ashpole, Ian Richardson and 12 others like this.

**Elaine Milne** Nope..... 😊
June 28 at 7:03am · Like

**Moshe Hadari** Shilly Hagish... 😊
June 28 at 7:06am via mobile · Unlike · 👍 2

**Elaine Milne** Aah....right...got it now. Must be because I'm Scottish 😊
June 28 at 7:07am · Unlike · 👍 2

**Patrick McEntee** Max Horne can do the voice over
June 28 at 7:16am via mobile · Unlike · 👍 1

**Max Horne** Us Shcotsh will never be shecond clash shitishens
June 28 at 7:27am · Unlike · 👍 2

**Moshe Hadari** One hears Sean' just isshued a shratement via hish shpokeshman- "Shimon, if you pershisht with this shillinesh, you will be isshued with a lishensh to shrill...
June 28 at 8:21am via mobile · Unlike · 👍 1

**Jonny Taffs** best one yet1
June 28 at 11:58am · Unlike · 👍 1

**Mark Ashpole** Great gag, it made me feel Shlightly shaken, but not stirred !
June 29 at 6:23am via mobile · Unlike · 👍 1

**29 June 2013** – 5 likes – left them a bit cold this one …

With the football (soccer) season still some weeks away, and in case any of you are missing it, over the next few days I propose some mildly (or more) amusing results from the LEAGUE of BANDS. All will become clear: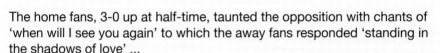

U2 – UB40

A record away win, where a rarely employed tactic saw the home team sink without trace. One in ten goals scored by Campbell.

**30 June 2013** – 4 likes – well, I liked it too

LEAGUE of BANDS:

Degrees 3 – Tops 4

The home fans, 3-0 up at half-time, taunted the opposition with chants of 'when will I see you again' to which the away fans responded 'standing in the shadows of love' ...

The away team then came back like a steam train, and are enjoying a well earned break in Acapulco.

**1 July 2013** – 7 likes

LEAGUE of BANDS:

Maroon 5 – Fun Boy 3

The home team won this with some very good moves (some say like Jagger) and though the away team used to be special, it is no longer true to say that it is what one does, as much as the way that one does it.

(So, we made it to July folks; back to a more traditional joke format tomorrow)

**2 July 2013** – 14 likes

Well, it is the second week of Wimbledon:
I asked 100 people if they could mime watching a game of tennis.
They all said no.

**3 July 2013** – some people are hard to please

**Simon Gibson**
July 3

I attended the funeral of a much loved 40 year old friend yesterday, who died when he was hit on the head with a tennis ball.

Very sad of course, but it was a lovely service.

Like · Comment · Promote · Share                    👍 20 💬 5 🚩 1

Greg Cummins, Ian Green, Julie Gibson and 17 others like this.

**Morwenna Clarke** Boom boom!!
July 3 at 6:55am · Unlike · 👍 1

**Moshe Hadari** Love(d by) all...
July 3 at 6:56am via mobile · Unlike · 👍 2

**Anthony Jones** love it !
July 3 at 10:00am · Unlike · 👍 1

**Julie Gibson** At last, one that made me laugh!
July 3 at 10:01pm via mobile · Like

**Ian Green** COME ON TIM!
July 4 at 7:23pm via mobile · Like

**4 July 2013** – I planned this months before,
and didn't get the reaction I hoped for – 5 likes

Has anyone worked out
Bruce Springsteen's nationality?

SG JOKE

**5 July 2013** – 6 likes

Le Tour is in full swing, so:
A pedestrian stepped off the pavement and into the road without looking, and promptly got knocked over by a passing cyclist.
"You were really lucky there," said the cyclist.
"What on earth are you talking about! That really hurt!" said the pedestrian, still on the pavement, rubbing his head. "How was I lucky?"
"Well" replied the cyclist, "I usually drive a bus!"

**6 July 2013** – I had a lie in and was chased by Anthony Jones, one of my biggest (though now much slimmer) fans – 11 likes and a share even ☺

**Simon Gibson**
July 6

I had another cycling joke lined up, but have had a "request", so here goes - good luck The Lions!!

An amateur rugby player from Cardiff is having a quiet drink in a Sydney Bar, a day or so ahead of the big game. He leans over to the bloke next to him and says, "Would you like to hear an Aussie joke?"

The fellow replies, "Well mate, before you tell that joke you should know something: I'm six feet tall, weigh 105kgs and I'm a Wallaby forward. The guy sitting next to me is 6'2", weighs 115kgs and he's an ex-Wallaby. Next to him is a bloke who's 6'5" weighs 120kgs and he's a current Wallaby second-row. Now, by all means, do you still want to tell that Aussie joke?"

The Welshman says, "Thanks for pointing that out. No, I won't be telling it - not if I'm going to have to explain it three times".

Like · Comment · Promote · Share          👍 11  💬 5  📤 1

David Pritchard, Mat Fogarty, Stevie Ray Plewes and 8 others like this.

**Katy Baxter** Hahaha!! x
July 6 at 8:47am via mobile · Like

**Simon Gibson** Anthony Jones I am sure you will recognise that this joke is normally at the expense of the Welsh, but in the interests of Lions unity ...
July 6 at 8:56am · Like · 👍 2

**Patrick McEntee** How do u keep a Welshman happy in Sydney just pick him
July 6 at 9:45am via mobile · Unlike · 👍 1

**Patrick McEntee** Now my fellow Lions let us support our team 100%
July 6 at 9:45am via mobile · Unlike · 👍 1

**Anthony Jones** Fantastic !!!
July 6 at 10:51am via mobile · Unlike · 👍 1

**7 July 2013** – 7 likes

Apparently yesterday's offering was a bit much for some of you, so:

The postman was early yesterday, so I opened the door in my pyjamas – until then, I didn't even know I had a door in my pyjamas!

**8 July 2013** – 11 likes

So, Andy Murray cleans up at Wimbledon – and this morning is named an honorary Womble by Great Uncle Bulgaria!

**9 July 2013** – 15 likes

Yesterday I got on a horse for the first time in around 30 years. What an experience!!

Everything was going really well until it started going quicker and I found myself out of control. I tried with all my might to hang on, but was thrown off.

Just when I thought things could not possibly get any worse, my foot got caught in the stirrup. As I fell, my head bounced harder and harder against the ground as the horse would neither stop nor slow down. I started to panic ... Then, just as I was giving up all hope, and about to lose consciousness, the manager of Tesco came and unplugged it.

**10 July 2013** – 13 likes

Tonight we will see a Waxing Crescent Moon, which reminds me – apparently, back in the 1970s, the Americans secretly built a restaurant on the Moon – only visited by astronauts, it is said that the food is brilliant, though it does lack any atmosphere ...

**11 July 2013** – 8 likes

Felt a little fresher yesterday.
This is a both a comment on the weather, locally, and .... my forecast
of the typical diary entry of a University student in late September.

**12 July 2013** – 12 likes

 **Simon Gibson**
July 12

There is a new restaurant in town - it's Indian, and last night I tried something I haven't had before - curried Toucan.

I must say, it was pretty much the best curry I have ever eaten, though the bill was enormous ...

(I have something a bit different for you, for the weekend ... see you on Saturday).

Like · Comment · Promote · Share                      👍 12  💬 5

Ian Richardson, Mark Hanna, Jacqueline Booth and 9 others like this.

 **Elaine Milne** Yes....I like! 🙂
July 12 at 7:02am · Unlike · 👍 2

 **Margaret Baxter** Hehe! x
July 12 at 7:55am via mobile · Unlike · 👍 2

 **Ian Foreman** I had a chicken tarka. its like chicken tikka....but it's a little otter......
July 12 at 8:11am · Unlike · 👍 2

 **Simon Gibson** Ian, you win a "virtual" prize - I have been waiting all year - see 17th January 🙂
July 12 at 8:22am · Like · 👍 1

 **Ian Foreman** I'm honoured, thank you. 🙂
July 12 at 8:45am via mobile · Unlike · 👍 1

Here's the plan. I put up a (short series of) 'what do you call a man' jokes and the challenge is to see how many you can (collectively) reply with - one each please. Here goes:

Q. What do you call a man with a plank on his head?
A. Edward.

Q. What do you call a man with two planks on his head?
A. Edward Wood.

Q. What do you call a man with three planks on his head?
A. Edward Woodward.

Q. What do you call a man with four planks on his head?
A. I don't know but Edward Woodward would.

And FINALLY ...

Q. Why does Edward Woodward have so many 'd's in his name?

(This is best said out loud, with the e said as an e, and war as in car ... you'll get it)

A. Because otherwise he'd be Ewar Woowar.

... and then some of the 18 other offers:

 **Elaine Milne** Almost... 😄 Here's my fave.... What do you call a fish without any eyes? Fsh...... 😄
July 13 at 7:28am · Unlike · 👍 3

 **Moshe Hadari** Q.What do you call a dog with no legs?
A. Does not matter.. He will not come...
July 13 at 11:07am via mobile · Unlike · 👍 2

 **Moshe Hadari** Q. What do you call...
A. Oh, damn.... This "one each, please..." rule sucks!!
July 13 at 11:19am via mobile · Unlike · 👍 1

 **David Wright** what do you call a man with binoculars ???? Seymour
July 13 at 12:52pm · Unlike · 👍 1

 **Mark Hanna** What do you call the man who graduates last in medical school? Doctor
July 13 at 2:02pm · Like

**Lee Clarke** What do you call a man with a seagull on his head?

Cliff

July 13 at 3:11pm via mobile · Unlike · 👍 2

 **Ravi Kumar** What do you call a man who puts others to work Simon Gibson

July 13 at 4:04pm · Unlike · 👍 3

 **John Mather** What do you call a man with no arms and no legs hanging on a wall? Art.

July 13 at 7:40pm · Like

 **John Mather** * What do you call a man who is lying down outside your front door?? -- Matt

* What do you call a man floating in your pool?? -- Bob

* What do you call a man sitting in a pile of leaves?? -- Russell

* What do you call a man with a shovel in his head?? -- Doug

 **Mark Ashpole** What do you call a man....up to his neck in a bog........Pete ( v. Sorry )

July 13 at 8:10pm via mobile · Unlike · 👍 1

 **Lee Clarke** What do you call a man with a car on his head.... Jack

July 13 at 8:17pm · Unlike · 👍 1

 **Lee Clarke** what do you call a man, who has never lived, has no idea about real life and absolutely no clue what financial advisers do? Compliance Officer.

July 13 at 8:20pm · Like

 **Lee Clarke** What do you call a very small man with a really large Rottweiler? "Sir"

July 13 at 8:21pm · Like

 **John Mather** What do you call a man who's been conned?

Mark.

What do you call a man who stabs people?

Dirk.

What do you call a man who prepare papers before death?

Will.

What do you call a man who's always looking for something?

Zeke.

July 13 at 8:21pm · Unlike · 👍 1

 **Mark Ashpole** What do you call a man who ..... Looks like a Bear ? ..... Ted

July 13 at 8:53pm via mobile · Unlike · 👍 1

**14 July 2013** – 5 likes

Here's the plan, part two ... 'what do you call a woman' jokes (keep them the right side of acceptable, please):

Q. What do you call a woman with a radiator on her head?
A. Anita.

**15 July 2013** – 12 likes and a share

What do you get if you cross a joke with a rhetorical question?

**16 July 2013** – 17 likes

Two pieces of black tarmac are standing chatting at the bar, when in walks a piece of red tarmac.

The piece of red tarmac demands a pint of bitter from the landlord in a really menacing manner, then downs it in one, slams his money on the bar and walks out. SILENCE.

The landlord turns to the two pieces of black tarmac and says ...

"Well, I am glad HE didn't cause any trouble – I've heard he's a bit of a cyclepath".

**17 July 2013** – 9 likes – thanks TC

Doctor, Doctor, I have come out in big red spots, like cherries on a cake.

You've got analogy.

**18 July 2013** – 11 likes and a share

Two British Gas engineers, a senior training supervisor and his rather younger trainee, were out checking meters in their local town. They parked their van at the end of the alley and worked their way to the other end, checking, noting and moving on methodically, house by house.

At the last house a 60-ish year old woman looking out of her kitchen window watched the two men as they checked her gas meter. Upon finishing, the senior engineer challenged his younger colleague to a race down the alley, back to the van, to prove that an older bloke could still outrun a younger one. The younger one accepted.

They set off at a fair old lick ...

As they came running up to the van, they realised that the lady from the last house was huffing and puffing along, not very far behind them. They stopped and asked her what was wrong.

Gasping for breath, she replied "When I see two gas men running as hard as you two were, I thought I'd better run too!"

**19 July 2013** – 9 likes

It's Friday, around the end of the school year and all is well. So, one to share - children love the slight naughtiness of this one, which though it is officially only 200/365 (WoW, 200!!), I have been telling for ... around 29 years ... according to my records.

Q. What do you call a man with a rabbit up his bum?

A. Warren.

**20 July 2013** – 10 likes

**Simon Gibson**
July 20

An elderly couple are in church. The wife leans over and whispers to her husband, "I just let out a long, silent fart. What should I do?"

The husband replies "First, replace the batteries in your hearing aid!"

Like · Comment · Promote · Share     👍 10 💬 5

Joy Haynes, Mark Ashpole, Stevie Ray Plewes and 7 others like this.

**Anthony Jones** That's went down a bomb over here !
July 20 at 10:03am via mobile · Unlike · 👍 1

**Henry Saltmarsh** Sorry Simon - not original today. ☹
July 20 at 10:40am · Like

**Simon Gibson** Henry, it hasn't been posted on my Facebook page by me this year, so it qualifies ... there has been some previous recycling - I never claimed I could write 365 new ones - hangs head in shame ☺
July 20 at 12:07pm · Like

**Anthony Jones** Simon, it's a cracker however old !
July 20 at 2:09pm via mobile · Unlike · 👍 1

**Ronnie Muhl** Classic!
July 20 at 2:35pm · Unlike · 👍 1

**21 July 2013** – 13 likes

A man walks into a library "May I have some fish and chips, please?" "This is a library" says a somewhat frustrated librarian.

"Sorry" says the man. "May I have some fish and chips, please?" he whispers.

**22 July 2013** – 16 likes and a new Prince (George)

A husband and wife were out shopping. The wife reminded her husband that her mother's birthday was coming up.

She said "Darling, can we look around for a birthday present for Mum? She wants something electric."

The husband replied "Of course we can. How about a chair?"

(For Elaine Milne and Phil Evans who share a birthday today - have a shockingly good one!)

**23 July 2013** – 10 likes and a few "yuks"

The tour bus is full of pensioners out on a long day trip. They seem in high spirits and are all looking forward to a great day. After a few miles, the driver gets a tap on the shoulder, and is handed several peanuts by a little old lady, which he gladly accepts and munches away on for a few minutes.

Soon afterwards, she again grabs his attention and hands him more peanuts, which again he eats.

When this happens for a third time he asks her "Why don't you eat the peanuts?"

"Oh" she replies. "We can't chew them because of our teeth. We just suck the chocolate off ..."

**24 July 2013** – 13 likes

Another sector of the UK economy comes out of recession, as a report from the Periscope Manufacturers Association says that business is looking up.

**25 July 2013** – 11 likes

So, now we know the new Prince is to be called George. This though  has thrown the press into a bit of a state – after all, this boy is born to be a King, and we've already had a period of British history known as 'Georgian'. What will they call his time?
Here then is my suggestion, and it is a bit of a Revolution. Let's not wait until he becomes King, let's show some love and pride now, let's go crazy, enjoy having a new Prince, and call it a Purple Reign ...

**26 July 2013** – 12 likes

I was in the supermarket yesterday and saw a couple wrapped in a barcode – I assume they were an item ...

**27 July 2013**– 7 likes

I remember the first video my Mum and Dad bought me after I got a VHS player. It was a day much like today, nothing special. When I opened it I thought it must be fantastic (and that Dad had chosen it) as it was in a completely plain box ... so exciting!

The title was very alluring – I remember that too ...

"Tape Head Cleaner"

... can't say I remember the plot or the storyline ...

(for those of a certain age, like Ian Green and Stevie Ray Plewes - happy birthday to both; may your memories never fade)

**28 July 2013** – 10 likes

I miss my school friend Jim. We went together to a recording of "Stars in their Eyes". I was only really there to support him, as he was going to be in the show!

The host got him on stage, asked him who he was going to be, Jim said "Glenn Miller" then he went though the mist ... and we never saw him again!

**29 July 2013** – 8 likes – and I thought this would be more appreciated

The darkest hour is before the dawn.
So, if you ARE going to steal your neighbour's milk, that's the time to do it!!

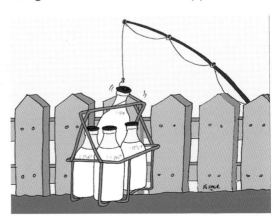

**30 July 2013** – 16 likes

Before you criticise someone, you should walk a mile in their shoes. This means that, when you do criticise them, you are a mile away ... and you have their shoes!

**31 July 2013** – bless you Elaine Milne

**Simon Gibson**
July 31

If at first you don't succeed ... might be best NOT to do that skydive.

(Seven months done, just five to do - ta da)

Like · Comment · Promote · Share          👍 15  💬 3

Ian Richardson, Anthony Jones, Mary Sinclair and 12 others like this.

> **Elaine Milne** Yeh, one skydive was enough for me, exactly on that basis 😉
> July 31 at 6:26am via mobile · Like

> **Simon Gibson** Elaine, I suspect you MAY have missed the point 😏
> July 31 at 6:26pm via mobile · Like

> **Elaine Milne** Sigh....not like me.... 😉
> July 31 at 6:31pm · Unlike · 👍 1

## AUGUST – HURRAH!!

**1 August 2013** – 21 likes

I have a passion for teaching children the value of money, and today I can even joke about it ...
A young lad enters a barber shop and the barber whispers to his customer, "This is the most stupid boy in the world. I'll prove it to you." The barber puts a pound in one hand and two 20 pence pieces in the other, then calls the boy over and asks, "Which do you want?" The boy takes the 20 pences and leaves. "What did I tell you?" said the barber. "That boy never learns!" Later, when the customer leaves, he sees the same boy coming out of the sweet shop. "Excuse me, son, may I ask you a question? Why did you take the 40 pence instead of the pound coin?"
The boy ate another sweet from his bag and replied, "Because the day I take the pound coin, the game is over!"

## 2 August 2013 – 9 likes

Late last night I went to a 24-hour store, one of those 'sells everything' places. When I got there, the owner was locking the front door. I said, "Hang on, the sign says you're open 24 hours."

He replied, "Not in a row!"

## 3 August 2013 – 9 likes

Welcome to the weekend ...

There was once a scientist named Berade who managed to create a giant, twenty-foot-tall pig, which he named after himself. Unfortunately, the pig's breath was really horrible.

The scientist also created seventy-six gorilla clones, and while he tried to replicate his pig experiment, to breed a better quality pig, he had the clones feed the pig over a hundred Cloret breath mints.

One day, the gorilla on mint duty spilled the mints, so the scientist began to beat it with a stick, at which point the clones simultaneously rebelled.

The police report said, "Seventy-six strong clones fed the pig Berade, with a hundred and ten Clorets close at hand."

## 4 August 2013 – 20 likes

A married couple were asleep when the telephone rang at 2am. The wife picked up the telephone, listened for a moment and then said, "How should I know? That's a good 60 miles from here." Then she hung up.

Her husband, now awake, says, "Who was that at 2 in the morning?"

His wife replies, "I don't know, some woman, wanting to know if the coast is clear ..."

## 5 August 2013 – 15 likes

After a couple of jokes in the last week that my own nine year old daughter deemed not fit for children, and at her request:

Exam Question: Please write, as precisely as possible, all you know about the great English watercolour artists of the eighteenth century.

Answer: They are all dead.

## 6 August 2013 – 23 likes – thanks Kate …

Bags of white sugar are very common in supermarkets, but bags of brown sugar?
Demerara.

## 7 August 2013 – 15 likes

Back to the topic of a couple of days ago.

I had the odd teacher like this ...

"Now children," said the teacher, as the ferry was about to leave Dover, bound for Calais. "What do we shout if a fellow pupil falls into the sea."

Up go a forest of hands – Tim gets chosen to answer. "Pupil overboard, sir."

"Quite right, very good," says the teacher. "And what do we shout if we see a teacher fall into the sea?"

"It depends which teacher, sir."

**8 August 2013** – 14 likes

Teacher: Can someone please give me a sentence starting with "I"?

Student: I is ...

Teacher: No, that doesn't work. Always say, "I am" ...

Student: All right, if you say so ... I am the ninth letter of the alphabet.

AND

**Simon Gibson**
August 8

Tomorrow is day 221/365 - and there will be news about 'plans' over the weekend ... thank you to everyone for your wonderful support - I see so many of you that never 'like' a joke but tell me you follow them religiously - does that mean you are praying for them to end? Well, after 31st December, you shall have your wish ...

Like · Comment · Promote · Share                                     4

**9 August 2013** – 5 likes and, well, 18 comments, mainly about not getting it!!

In that wonderful, classic film, E.T., what is E.T. short for?

He only as little legs.
(I know, I missed out the H of has and all hell broke loose ...)

**10 August 2013** – 18 likes and very nearly an (unintended) repeat joke

Here goes with the big day. Joke first (two more posts to follow):

A horse walks into a smart cocktail bar in Newmarket (it's OK, if you are local, I know).

The doorman says to the horse, "You can't come in here without a tie on."

The horse goes out to his car (!), looks in the boot and gets out a set of jump leads, which he ties around his neck.

He goes back in and says to the man, "This OK...?"

The doorman says, "Hmm, I suppose so ... but don't be starting anything."

**Also on 10 August:**

**Simon Gibson** shared a link.
August 10

Part two:

Today at 5.55pm at Newmarket's July Course, the Reg Day Memorial Handicap will be run under the name of Alzheimer's Research UK. I have sponsored the race for them for the next three years, for reasons most of you will know.

We sent the Press Association the story earlier this week and they (very kindly) circulated it across the UK - it has been reported on in almost every county of England via regional newspapers, and in The Scotsman, which alone has a circulation of 30,000. You can read more via this link - it would be great to get ARUK more publicity, so please do share this post:

http://www.alzheimersresearchuk.org/news-detail/10834/Newmarket-horse-race-named-after-UKs-leading-dementia-research-charity/

pas for fundraising

**A horse race at Newmarket has been named after Alzheimer's Research UK.**
www.alzheimersresearchuk.org

A horse race Newmarket's July Course will be renamed in support of the UK's leading dementia research charity, Alzheimer's Research UK.

**AND:**

### 11 August 2013 – 11 likes

Now that I have your attention ... quick pole:

North ... or ... South?

### 12 August 2013 – 10 likes

So I don't let you down while away, I have been planning 14 for the upcoming family holiday – here is one that did not make that list, perhaps for obvious reasons ...

I was arguing with my wife about holidays the other day.

I want to go to Istanbul ...

... she wants to come with me.

**13 August 2013** – 9 likes

I mentioned my wife in a slightly unfavourable light yesterday, so now I turn on me ...

There's no harm in the truth, is there?

Well ...

I was so ugly when I was born, the midwife slapped my mother.

Twice.

**14 August 2013** – 19 likes

I was approached by a policeman yesterday. He handed me a pencil and a very large, very thin piece of paper. Apparently I have to help him trace someone ...

**15 August 2013** – 6 likes

I am friendly with a bloke who is on a personal crusade for fat people.

I hate being this close to a wide supremacist ...

**16 August 2013** – 12 likes

My Uncle Tommy mends windows. He nowadays specialises in 17th and 18th Century, exceptionally intricate and ornamental stuff, sometimes called Baroque. I say nowadays because when he started doing it 40 years ago he used to do any old sort of window that needed work. However, no matter what sort of job he did, however brilliantly he sorted out the glass work, customers never seemed happy to pay his bill, claiming, more often than not, "it is not worth the money, I can buy a new one for that" ...

So, if any of you have the right sort of windows and need a real specialist, look up my Uncle Tommy on the Internet or in Yellow Pages – he is easy to find. He uses his corporate strapline, honed over the years, like all excellent marketing and branding, to simply tell people all about him in a line. Just look up ...

"If it ain't Baroque, don't fix it."

**17 August 2013**– 8 likes

To celebrate the news of an important date for Josh, I have written a limerick which I am sure Bazza Haynes will read to you with great relish. Here goes:

There once was a fellow from Goring
Who was often described as, well, boring
Except for the times
He played nursery rhymes
With his body, by farting and snoring

(The nine year old here thinks Baa Baa Black Sheep would make a good one to pretend to do, unless of course anyone out there can actually fart/snore a nursery rhyme, in which case, please put on YouTube!!)

Finally, Mum already a bit bored by the constant family attempts to bring Dad's limerick to life ...

**18 August 2013** – 13 likes

We are off on our family holiday today, which reminds me ...

This chap is on safari in Africa when he comes across an elephant lying on the ground, apparently in distress. He investigates and finds it has a thorn in its foot.

He removes it (the thorn, not the foot) and the elephant trots happily away.

Twenty years on, and the same man is standing in the street in London watching a circus procession pass by. When the elephant gets level with him, it stops, looks straight at him, reaches out with its trunk, lifts him bodily into the air ...

... then smashes him on the ground and jumps on him. It was a different elephant.

**19 August 2013** – 10 likes

It's all going off here in Scarborough:

Local Police are looking for a man with one eye – typical inefficiency.

**20 August 2013** – 10 likes

Last night we were in a restaurant and a very loud fellow guest started to draw attention to himself. Then we noticed he had some custard in one ear and some jelly in the other. That's right ...

... he was a trifle deaf.

**21 August 2013** – 16 likes

Doctor: Do you know what is wrong with you?

Me: Yes Doctor, I am having trouble pronouncing my Fs, Ts and Hs.

Doctor: Well, you can't say fairer than that then ...

THEN, just some reported truth got 7 likes – it is funny though:
Woman on the beach, Scarborough, today, reading from the newspaper: It says that eating avocado burns fat from round your middle. I eat avocado every day.

Thinks to self: no doubt you do, but if you put down the four donuts you currently have balanced in one hand, and the chips in the other, that might mean the avocado has a CHANCE!!

**22 August 2013** – 13 likes

More excitement in Scarborough last night – I saw a bloke running (well, staggering) out of a pub with a fruit machine on his back.

I thought, "He's taking a gamble."

**Simon Gibson**
August 23 near Scarborough, England

Sometimes they just come to me. Yesterday's local paper (story embellished for comedic purposes, headline genuine):

A tourist, unfamiliar with Peasholm Park, became trapped on the central island after hours when his wife went home without him and in a desperate attempt to escape, and after a glass too many of Claret, fell into the industrial size tins that the Council use to paint their floating pagoda deep red. That's right, he was ...

Like · Comment · Unfollow Post · Promote · Share

Margaret Baxter, Stevie Ray Plewes, Rachel Levitt and 5 others like this.

**24 August 2013** – 19 likes, but not Aunty Mary, my wife's biggest fan …

My wife and I always hold hands on holiday. If I let go, she shops.

**25 August 2013** – 10 likes

Whilst out shopping yesterday, I thought I would buy something for my wife, so I went to the lingerie department in M&S.

'I need a new bra for my wife', I said to the assistant.
'Certainly Sir', she said, 'What bust?'
'Nothing, it's just worn out.'

(My 'real' wife assures me that I will 'pay for' his 'joke' bra - well, she deserves a treat … oh, hang on … )

**26 August 2013** – 18 likes

I had a ploughman's lunch yesterday – he was livid.

**27 August 2013** – 8 likes

We had a marvellous day at the beach yesterday, when we 'caught' a fish and a crab … which reminds me:

Give a man a fish and he will eat for a day. Teach him how to fish …
… and he will sit in a boat all day, drinking beer.

**28 August 2013** – 10 likes

Most of you won't know this about me, but I have a huge seashell collection. My main problem is where to keep it. At the moment …

… I keep it scattered on beaches all over the world.

**29 August 2013** – 17 likes

The world is going mad!
I see that eBay has a listing: Dead budgie for sale.
It's not going cheap …

## 30 August 2013 – 23 likes

**Simon Gibson**
August 30

Just got a text from my Grandad, which is worrying, as he never sends texts. Hang on, is that an 'I' or an 'O'?

Oh, thanks goodness, it's an 'I' ...

... for a moment there I thought he had shot himself ...

Like · Comment · Promote · Share

Anthony Jones, Margaret Baxter, Mark Cross and 20 others like this.

**Mandi Plummer** Back up to the usual standard
August 30 at 1:48pm · Unlike · 1

**Margaret Baxter** Hehehehe! We're scraping each other off the floor! X
August 30 at 8:50pm via mobile · Unlike · 1

**Anthony Jones** Love it
August 31 at 5:36am · Unlike · 1

## 31 August 2013 – 12 likes

When I struggled to read Grandad's text yesterday, I decided to go to see an optician.

'Have you ever had your eyes checked?', he asked.

I replied, 'No, they have always been this colour ...'

END of another month ☺

**1 September 2013** – 3 likes – WHY only THREE??

As we finish our holiday in North Yorkshire, it has come to my attention that the local council are employing an Irishman to write their road signs.

I do not know this for certain, it's a bit of a guess – see what you think; here's one we spotted:

That was a bad bend, wasn't it!

**2 September 2013** – 16 likes

Back home and ready for work and there is a tap on the front door …

Our plumber has a strange sense of humour!

**3 September 2013** – 15 likes

Two cannibals eating a clown – one turns to the other and says …

"Does this taste funny to you?"

**4 September 2013** – 20 likes

The boy comes home from his first day at school.

Mum asks, "What did you learn today?"

He replies, "Not enough. I have to go back tomorrow."

**5 September 2013** – 11 likes

My Grandma was a very sage old lady.

She never minded my Grandad chasing after pretty girls, late in life.

As she said, their dog used to chase cars, but he couldn't drive!

**6 September 2013** – 14 likes

It turns out infertility is not hereditary.

## 7 September 2013 – 14 likes

If you have a teenager in your life, especially a daughter, and you can't get them off their iPhone, iPod or iPad, well, here's an idea.

Introduce them to the iRon!

## 8 September 2013 – 23 likes

I tried to catch fog yesterday. Mist.

## 9 September 2013 – 15 likes for the joke … a share …

Ladies, I have some important news for you – here are the five golden rules when it comes to men - you can thank me later:
1. You must find a man who will love you, cherish you, do anything for you;
2. You need a man who keeps himself clean and tidy, who believes in the same for a home;
3. You must find a man that is sufficiently wealthy that, whilst it may not be money no object, he doesn't have to think twice about treating you;
4. You must find a man that is a great lover, that can satisfy your needs; and most importantly of all …
…
5. You must NEVER let these four men meet!

… then this which set up the next few days:

## 10 September 2013 – 16 likes and the start of a mini limerick-fest

Here comes the first of a few home written limericks on subjects suggested by you, the audience. I hope they amuse/entertain ...

The Olympics are heading to Tokyo
Where people will run, jump and even throw
Excitement a'plenty
Come late 2020
Just not for this athlete, I'm REALLY slow!

## 11 September 2013 – 7 likes, comments and a share!

Limerick II - not exactly Harry Potter, but threatening to become a series.

A wonderful place is South Wales
By jove, I could tell you some tales!
I could, but I daren't
You see, I'm a parent
And children can't visit in jails!

Tomorrow, the humble prawn ...

## 12 September 2013 – 12 likes

Now it's the time of the prawn
And some hope that a limerick 'twill spawn
It is tricky, of course
But with Marie Rose sauce
Is a 70s cocktail reborn

## 13 September 2013 – 13 likes

A wonderful flower the rose is
The scent a real joy to the nose is
Their colours are many
Names, ten a penny
And it's here that this limerick closes

## PLUS

I was given one more rhyming word
I think it's a cat; never purred
Yes, there's often much fuss
'Bout ye olde platypus
Duck-billed, beaver-tailed AND furred!

## AND finally ...

There once was a bloke from Newmarket
Who had an old car – couldn't park it!
Driving gloves and a jumper
Bashed body and bumper
Not the car, the bloke from Newmarket

**14 September 2013** – 18 likes

Today's joke is themed, and is with the permission of the current Mrs Gibson, with whom I celebrate a wedding anniversary this very day. It's a joke folks – here goes:

If "I am" is the shortest sentence in the English language, then the longest must be "I do" ...

**15 September 2013** – 13 likes

Latest food scandal hits Tesco – mule meat found in their muffins.

**16 September 2013** – 21 likes

Here in Chicago, it really did rain cats and dogs yesterday.

I stepped in a poodle.

**17 September 2013** – 21 likes

Just landed at Heathrow and I really have got to get back to my little boy – when I left on Saturday, we were in the middle of a game of hide and seek!!

**18 September 2013** – 11 likes

Why do bakers hate sarcasm?

Because it is the lowest form of wheat ...

**19 September 2013** – didn't go according to plan – just 7 likes for the original joke, but then …

I am honoured and also in a bit of a quandry. I have been invited to do an after dinner speech for Chelsea FC this Saturday ... and only 30 minutes after that invitation arrived I was asked to go and do a gig for Sunderland FC.

What to do? Two great opportunities, and I don't want to let either of them down.

Hang on, I have an idea – as they are BOTH described as 'End of Season' events, perhaps I could suggest they combine them, and that way I won't let anyone down ...

Blast, had a special joke planned for today and completely forgot about it – the football took over and look where that got me – oh well, tomorrow morning (early) it is then ...

## 20 September 2013 – 11 likes

Well, what an opportunity missed yesterday. It was International Talk Like A Pirate Day (yes, really, me hearties, 19th September – put it in yer diary for next year) and here's what I had planned for weeks, only to forget it!

Why are pirates called pirates?

Because they aaaarrrrggghhh!

## 21 September 2013 – 16 likes

Johnny Depp has taken up yoga, big time. Apparently he likes doing it in character, as Captain Jack Sparrow.

Don't worry if you can't imagine that – you can buy his new DVD, from Monday:

Pilates of the Caribbean.

## 22 September 2013 – 16 likes

Yesterday I won 17 games of Rock, Paper, Scissors in a row.

Well, I was playing against the somewhat predictable Edward Scissorhands

**23 September 2013** – 13 likes

The animal rights bloke that has stolen my milk producing pet has really annoyed me.

That's right - he's got my goat ...

**24 September 2013** – 13 likes as our young friend Josh went into hospital for a big operation

Q: What do you call a dinosaur that never gives up?

A: Try and try and try and try-seratops.

(and especially for Josh, an extra 'good luck' dinosaur joke:

Q: Why can't you hear a pterodactyl using the toilet?

A: Because the p is silent.)

**25 September 2013** – 10 likes

'Dr, Dr, I think I need glasses.'

'You certainly do Sir, this is a petrol station.'

**26 September 2013** – 13 likes and comments

**Simon Gibson**
September 26

(Especially for Josh, to aid his recovery - Bazza Haynes you have to tell him this and make it realistic when you get to the punchline - the nurses will love it ...)

'Dr, Dr, I feel like a pig.'

'How long have you felt like a pig?'

'Oh, for about a weeeeeeeeeeeeeek!'

Like · Comment · Promote · Share                    👍 13 💬 4

Keith Grimsey, Mark Ashpole, Ian Richardson and 10 others like this.

**Bazza Haynes** Not a problem Simon, will let him have the full works soon..lol..☺
September 26 at 6:43am · Unlike · 👍 1

**Mary Sinclair** God one
September 26 at 7:26am · Like

**Mary Sinclair** even good one!
September 26 at 7:26am · Unlike · 👍 1

**Mark Ashpole** And I was expecting the old.... Try Taking this Oinkment...... Keep them coming Si.
September 26 at 6:37pm via mobile · Unlike · 👍 1

**27 September 2013** – 8 likes

'Dr, Dr, I feel really poorly.'

'What are the symptoms?'

'Um, yellow people, on a US cartoon show?'

(Keep smiling Josh)

**28 September 2013** – 15 likes

'Dr, Dr, help, I swallowed a bone!'

'Are you choking?'

'No, I really did swallow a bone ...'

**29 September 2013** – 20 likes

'Dr, Dr, everyone keeps calling me average.'

'That's just mean.'

**30 September 2013** – 20 likes

When I was ready to pay for my purchases at Tesco on Saturday, the cashier said, "Strip down, facing me!"

Making a mental note to complain to Head Office about local staff taking liberties, I nevertheless did just as she instructed.

When the hysterical shrieking had finally subsided, I realised that she was referring to my credit card.

I have been asked to shop elsewhere in future. As if Waitrose will have me now ...

**1 October 2013** – 24 likes

I've been doing some online 'browsing' and there is a nice offer on at Amazon – if you buy all of Adam & The Ants' sheet music, they'll throw in a stand & deliver.

## 2 October 2013 – 23 likes

A frog goes to see a fortune teller to find out if he will ever be lucky with the opposite sex.

The fortune teller reads his palm (imagine it) and tells the frog, "I have some good news and I have some bad news. Which would you like to hear first?"

In time honoured tradition (at least that's how jokes work) the frog asks for the good news first.

The fortune teller says, "You are going to meet a very pretty girl who is going to want to know all about you."

"Great," says the frog. "I can't wait. What's the bad news?"

"The bad news is you're going to meet her in a biology class," replies the fortune teller.

## 3 October 2013 – 18 likes and a share!

George was keen to buy a pet, and in the end he spent a lot of money at his local pet store on a talking centipede which came in a small box.

Excited to show off his new pet to his friends, George asked the centipede (in the box) if he'd like to go out to the bar for a drink.

There was no answer from the box. George began to wonder if his talking centipede could actually talk - had he been sold a dud?

Impatiently, he put his face up close to the box and shouted, "Hello! Would you like to go out for a drink with me?"

A little voice came from the box ...

"I heard you the first time – I am putting my shoes on."

**4 October 2013** – 19 likes

Visibility wasn't good the other day, and I got pulled over by a traffic policeman after driving at around 70mph.

He asked, "So, Sir, what would you do if Mr. Fog came down suddenly?"

"I would put Mr. Foot on Mr. Brake," I replied sarcastically.

"Let me start again," he sighed, "What would you do if mist or fog came down suddenly?"

**5 October 2013** – 11 likes

I was naughty when I was younger and one day I stood on the shoulders of two vampire friends so I could steal a couple of things from a top shelf.

I was arrested for shoplifting ... on two counts.

**6 October 2013** – 9 likes

My Aunty Joan has been feeling bloated and bunged up and hasn't been able to go to the loo for several days – I rang her and said, 'Are you taking anything for it?'

'Yes', came the reply ...

... 'usually some knitting and the Sunday papers'.

**7 October 2013** – 16 likes

I rang my Mum yesterday to tell her I have bought a theatre. 'I am planning the first show before Christmas', I told her.

'Are you having me on?!', she asked?

'Well, you can have an audition, but I'm not promising anything ...'

## 8 October 2013 – 14 likes

On the day we are warned that there may be electricity shortages this winter:

Two atoms are walking down the street – one says to the other, 'Oh no, I've lost an electron!'

'Are you sure?', asks the other.

'Yes', says the first one ... 'I am positive.'

## 9 October 2013 – 19 likes

At the end of a recent job interview, our HR Manager asked the prospective candidate if they had an ideal salary. Straight from Cambridge University, and undoubtedly with excellent credentials, the response was, 'Well, I thought £147,000 ... depending on the benefits.'

'How does eight weeks holiday, life cover of four times your salary, a contributory pension, medical insurance and a new car every three years (leased) – let's say a Jaguar for the first one - sound?' responds the HR Manager.

'Wow. That's amazing. You must be kidding!!', says the interviewee ...

'Yes, I am, but you started it ...'

## 10 October 2013 – 11 likes

What is black and white and eats like a horse?

A zebra.

**11 October 2013** – 12 likes

Lollipop stick or not, I shall persevere ...

What is small, red and whispers?

A hoarse radish.

**12 October 2013** – 10 likes

Something bad happens to water when they bottle it. Read the label ...

'This water has been flowing through the xx hills (I don't want to be sued) for thousands of years, gathering minerals and other great stuff that is naturally good for you etc. etc.' .....

.... then the label tells us, wisely, 'drink before 29th November.'

**13 October 2013** – 11 likes

Based on the weather, today's the day we've all been saving for ... so to cheer me up, here's a joke:

Freddy got a job as a TV weatherman in the Far East.

Unfortunately, try as he might, he never got a single forecast right.

Eventually he was fired and got the plane home.

On arrival, a friend asks why he is back so soon.

Freddy replies, 'The climate didn't agree with me.'

**14 October 2013** – 19 likes

I don't know about you, but in future I am going to put ALL my eggs in one basket. That way, I won't look such a fool walking around Sainsbury's ...

**15 October 2013** – 9 likes

Breaking news: Vigil held overnight in Manchester.

I don't know where the other Thunderbirds are. Anyone?

**16 October 2013** – 14 likes

Q. What do you call someone who points out the obvious?

A. Someone who points out the obvious.

**17 October 2013** – 15 likes

Hedgehogs. What is it with not sharing the hedges, guys?

**18 October 2013** – 23 likes

Yesterday I was attacked by a man who threw a bottle of Omega 3 tablets at me.

Don't panic, it's OK, I only suffered ...

... super fish oil injuries.

**19 October 2013** – 12 likes

Q. What is the first rule of grammar?

A. Double negatives are a no-no.

**20 October 2013** – 9 likes

Q. What is the first letter of the alphabet?

A.

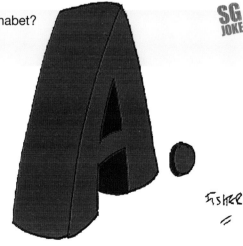

SG
JOKE

Fisher

**21 October 2013** – 16 likes for one of my own jokes!!

News from the world of show business. Apparently, Beyoncé has a nasty nerve infection, and it's also affected her speech. She plans to raise money for unmarried women who have been similarly affected.

All the shingle ladies ...

**22 October 2013** – my wonderful wife's 40th birthday – so this

**Simon Gibson**
October 22

Today is my amazing wife's birthday, so, as it would be wrong to have this pass without suitable comment:

I bought a ticket for the National Lottery this Saturday - my wife asked me, if I won, would I still love her.

'Of course I would', I replied.

'I'd miss you, but I'd still love you!'

Like · Comment · Promote · Share

Ian Bedford, Joy Haynes, Mark Ashpole and 19 others like this.

**23 October 2013** – 15 likes

I ordered some goods online the other day and it cost me an arm and a leg.

Turns out I used my donor card instead of my credit card.

**24 October 2013** – 14 likes

Rehearsals for the panto (Robyn Hood, 28th to 30th November) are in full swing ... which reminds me:

When I was a boy, our family was very poor. Dad tried supplementing his income by taking a job as a contortionist ... but still couldn't make ends meet.

**25 October 2013** – 19 likes

The Sergeant-Major barked at the young soldier, "I didn't see you at camouflage training this morning."

"Thank you very much, Sir."

**26 October 2013** – 9 likes for the intended joke

Two professors are chatting, sitting outside at a nudist colony (as you do; what's the point of sitting inside).

The history professor asks his companion, "Have you read Marx?"

The psychology professor replies, "Yes. I think it's from the wicker chairs."

PLUS, 5 for this overheard: Genius!

In Cambridge and Big Issue seller says to guy who is graduating today, 'by 12 o'clock you'll qualify to do this' ...

**27 October 2013** – 6 likes

Day 300 folks! I think I need to do a joke about clocks (about time I hear you say) ...

The clocks went back last night – I love it when that happens – it means the clock in my car will be right for the next six months!

**28 October 2013** – 9 likes

Dinner with MC Hammer and Chico last night. You cannot believe the carnage – all I asked was whether anyone had the time ...

**29 October 2013** – 7 likes

Halloween minus 2:

Robots are NEVER afraid – nerves of steel.

## 30 October 2013 – 15 likes

**Simon Gibson**
October 30

Halloween minus 1:

In the run up to Halloween, a slightly ghoulish display is planned at the local museum - skeletons of murder victims from Victorian times. How will it work?

Remains to be seen …

Like · Comment · Promote · Share

Simon Greenwood, Ian Richardson, Margaret Baxter and 12 others like this.

**Mary Sinclair** Very good!
October 30 at 8:06am · Unlike · 👍 1

**Simon Gibson** Thanks Mary - not so sure what you'll say about my offering tomorrow …
October 30 at 8:38am · Like

**Phil Evans** Magical play on words 😃
October 30 at 8:42am via mobile · Unlike · 👍 1

## 31 October 2013 – 12 likes

**Simon Gibson**
October 31

Welcome to Halloween - an expensive time if you have three children, but I have the advantage (here comes the backlash from the Aunts, Great-Aunts, etc.) of having UGLY CHILDREN.

If you also have ugly children, here is a money saving tip.

Instead of buying expensive masks before they go trick or treating, just buy elastic bands and stretch between their ears. 😃

(Retreats to a safe distance) …

Like · Comment · Promote · Share

Mark Hanna, Julie Gibson, Elaine Milne and 9 others like this.

## 1 November 2013 – 21 likes

Three nouns, three adjectives, two verbs and a conjunction appeared in court on Thursday.

They are due to be sentenced next week.

## 2 November 2013 – 17 likes

I refuse to talk to our milkman, as he has less than 10 toes.

That's right, I am lack toes intolerant ...

## 3 November 2013 – 11 likes

I was in love with posh spice when I was younger.

Ended up spending a fortune every week on saffron.

## 4 November 2013 – 19 likes

I received an email yesterday from someone trying to sell me Mount Everest for £10 million.

I told him I thought it was a bit steep.

## 5 November 2013 – 11 likes

I have discovered that the good thing about lending out my time machine is that I get it back pretty much immediately!

## 6 November 2013 – 18 likes

Delighted to say that my friend who fell into an upholstery machine has fully recovered.

## 7 November 2013 – 22 likes

**Simon Gibson**
November 7

Imagine a chicken dancing across the road.

Poultry in motion.

Like · Comment · Promote · Share                    👍22 💬2

Simon Greenwood, Ian Bedford, Henry Saltmarsh and 19 others like this.

**Anthony Jones** Love it
November 7 at 9:06am via mobile · Unlike · 👍1

**Mary Catherine Taylor** "Strictly" the best...
November 7 at 6:45pm via mobile · Unlike · 👍1

## 8 November 2013 – 17 likes

Amazing! Yesterday, there was a strike at work. Really ...

After waiting years, FINALLY someone turns up who actually knows how to ten-pin bowl ...

## 9 November 2013 – 12 likes

Argon walks into a bar and orders a drink.

The bartender says, "Sir, we don't serve noble gasses."

There was no reaction.

## 10 November 2013 – 15 likes

For the physicists among you that love Marvel comics (a select audience), and especially for those of you that only read my jokes periodically:

If the Silver Surfer and Iron Man teamed up to take on evil, they would be alloys ...

**11 November 2013** – 7 likes

HeHe.

I just found two isotopes of Helium.

**12 November 2013** – 10 likes

I do think it's cute when lovers carve their names into a tree.

That bit I get.

I also think taking a knife on a date is a bit weird ...

**13 November 2013** – 15 likes

What causes anaphylactic shock?

I can give you that in a nutshell.

**14 November 2013** – 16 likes

What is the world coming to?

I remember the days when 'Blue Ray' was nothing more complicated than an elderly man in our village who regularly used to expose himself ...

**15 November 2013** – 13 likes

Sponsoring the Lavenham Literary Festival this weekend, so:

Yesterday, I went to the local bookshop to buy a book about conspiracies. There weren't any. Coincidence? I don't think so ...

**16 November 2013** – 10 likes

Inspired by the literary festival, I went back to the local bookshop to buy a 'Where's Wally' book, and couldn't find one anywhere.

Well played Wally!

**17 November 2013** – 17 likes

I remember when our son set fire to one of his Mr Men books.

No more Mr Nice Guy.

**18 November 2013** – 18 likes

Little Johnny's primary school class was on a field trip to the police station where they saw pictures, pinned to a notice board, of the 10 most wanted criminals locally.

One of the youngsters pointed to a picture and asked if it really was the photo of a wanted person. "Yes," said the policeman. "The detectives want very badly to capture him."

Little Johnny asked, "Why didn't you keep him when you took his picture then?"

**Simon Gibson**
November 19 near Cambridge

That's what friends are for:

"Hello, is this the FBI?"
"Yes. What do you want?"
"I am calling to report my neighbour John Smith. He is hiding marijuana inside his winter firewood."
"Thank you very much for the call, sir. We will get on it immediately."

The next day, agents descend on John's house. They search the shed where the firewood is kept. Using axes, they chop open every piece of wood, but find no marijuana. They swear at John and then leave, grumpily.

The phone rings at John's house later that day.
"Hey, John. Did the FBI come?"
"Yes, they did!"
"Did they chop your firewood?"
"They did."

"Happy Birthday my friend!"

Like · Comment · Promote · Share                    👍 19  💬 2  📄 1

Mark J Hassall, Keith Grimsey, Ian Richardson and 16 others like this.

**Morwenna Clarke** LOL!!
November 19 at 7:26am · Unlike · 👍 1

**Ian Richardson** Really like this one!
November 19 at 8:30pm via mobile · Unlike · 👍 1

## 20 November 2013 – 26 likes and a share

On a bitterly cold winter evening, a bit like last night, a wife sent her husband a text message ...

"Windows frozen".

The husband responded, "Pour some warm water over them."

Some time later he received the following text from his wife:

"The computer has stopped working completely now."

(Any similarity to people you know is purely coincidental!)

## 21 November 2013 – 17 likes

One night, a group of chess enthusiasts checked into the Castle Hotel, and were standing in the lobby discussing their recent tournament victories.

After about an hour, the manager, Mr Bishop, came out of his office, walking at an angle, and asked them to disperse.

"But why," asked one of their number, Mr King, as they moved off, some in odd directions, him, a single step at a time.

"Because," said Mr Bishop, "I can't stand chess-nuts boasting in an open foyer."

**22 November 2013** – 12 likes

As we prepare for Dr Who day tomorrow, celebrating the 50th anniversary of the BBC TV drama, one "Dr, but not that Dr, and not a Doctor, Doctor" joke:

Philip: "Doctor, I had the worst dream of my life last night. I dreamt I was with 12 of the most beautiful chorus girls in the world. Blondes, brunettes, redheads, all dancing in a row, all gorgeous."

Doctor: "To be honest, that doesn't sound so terrible. How can I help?"

Philip: "Well, in the dream, I was the third girl from the left."

**23 November 2013** – 21 likes

People have waited fifty years – so I thought fans deserve more than one joke today ...

For all the Whovians, on the Day of the Doctor:

Q. What happens when one Doctor meets another Doctor when travelling back in time?
A. It's a pair-a-docs ...

Q. What does the Doctor eat with his spaghetti bolognese?
A. Dalek bread ...

Q. Who was the scariest time lord?
A. Doctor Boo!

Q. When the Doctor last escaped from the Daleks, he came out with very soft skin - why was that?
A. Ex-fo-li-ate, ex-fo-li-ate ...

## 24 November 2013 – 4 likes – what is it about Sundays??

From last night:
"Great men are forged in fire, it is the privilege of lesser men to light the flame", Dr Who.

In a joint press release from their agents, Adele, Bruce Springsteen and Billy Joel said:

"The rain is on fire, I'm on fire (as are the streets) but we didn't start the fire".

In a further statement, representatives of The Doors and The Prodigy announced:

"It was us".

## 25 November 2013 – 6 likes

Make it idiot proof, and someone will make a better idiot. Probably Apple.

The iDiot ... start it up and it will pull you down to its level, then beat you with its experience ... may I have the rights to this iDea, please?

## 26 November 2013 – 15 likes

Don't take this personally ...

He who laughs last ... thinks slowest.

## 27 November 2013 – 14 likes

If one synchronised swimmer drowns ... do the others have to?

## 28 November 2013 – 8 likes

I intend to live forever – so far, so good.

**29 November 2013** – 24 likes

There was recently a prison break and I happened to be nearby –
I spotted a midget climb up the perimeter fence.

As he then jumped down he sneered at me and I thought ...

"... that's a little condescending".

**30 November 2013** – 14 likes

I must be ill. I thought I saw a German sausage flying past my
window – it was actually a seabird. That's right ...

I've taken a tern for the wurst ...

**1 December 2013** – 15 likes and 1 share

My friend is a bit of a DIY disaster area, and he never asks for help.

Recently, he got crushed by a pile of books.

He's only got his shelf to blame.

(Talking of books, I am on the final chapter, just December to go, so now
the count is 1/31)

**2 December 2013** – 19 likes and 1 share

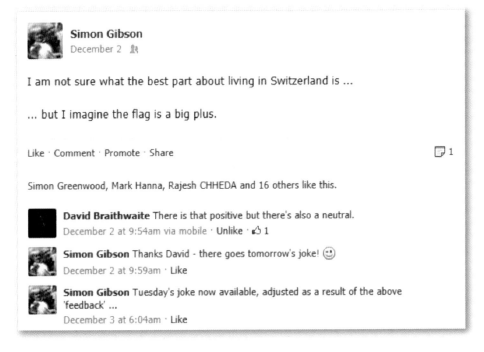

**Simon Gibson**
December 2

I am not sure what the best part about living in Switzerland is ...

... but I imagine the flag is a big plus.

Like · Comment · Promote · Share                                    1

Simon Greenwood, Mark Hanna, Rajesh CHHEDA and 16 others like this.

**David Braithwaite** There is that positive but there's also a neutral.
December 2 at 9:54am via mobile · Unlike · 1

**Simon Gibson** Thanks David - there goes tomorrow's joke! :)
December 2 at 9:59am · Like

**Simon Gibson** Tuesday's joke now available, adjusted as a result of the above 'feedback' ...
December 3 at 6:04am · Like

**3 December 2013** – 6 likes and described by one follower as the best yet!! 6 likes mind you

Still on flags ...

Q. What is red, white, blue ... and yellow?

A. The star-spangled banana!

**4 December 2013** – 20 likes

Whilst out shopping in Vienna, I saw a man with one arm, browsing in the second hand shop.

Optimistic ...

## 5 December 2013 – 19 likes

A tourist in Vienna is going through a graveyard and suddenly he hears some music. No one is about, so he starts searching for the source. He finally locates the origin and finds it is coming from a grave with a headstone that reads:

Ludwig van Beethoven, 1770 – 1827.

Then he realises that the music is the Ninth Symphony and it is being played backwards.

Puzzled, he leaves the graveyard and persuades a friend to return with him. By the time they arrive back at the grave, the music has changed. This time it is the Seventh Symphony, and like the previous piece, it is being played backwards. Curious, the men agree to consult a music scholar.

When they return with the expert, the Fifth Symphony is playing, again backwards.

The expert notices that the symphonies are being played in the reverse order in which they were composed, the 9th, then the 7th, then the 5th. By the next day word has spread and a throng has gathered around the grave. They are all listening to the Second Symphony being played backwards. Just then the graveyard's caretaker ambles up to the group. Someone in the group asks him if he has an explanation for the music.

"Don't you get it?" the caretaker says, incredulously.

"It's Beethoven", ...

"He's decomposing".

## 6 December 2013 – 14 likes

Q. What do you get if you cross a christmas tree with an iPad?

A. A pineapple.

## 7 December 2013 – 15 likes

Things are a bit tough this year – just wrapped up my son's Christmas present - four AA batteries ... with a note:
"Toys not included".

**8 December 2013** – 8 likes (well, I liked it!)

More preparations for the festive season in our house today.

Going out shortly to post pictures of really angry mice to relatives and loved ones.

Yes, the cross-mouse cards are finished ...

**9 December 2013** – 12 likes

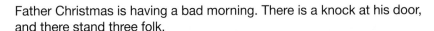

Father Christmas is having a bad morning. There is a knock at his door, and there stand three folk.

"Your names?", he asks.

"Presley", says one.
"Costello", the second one replies.
"Perkins", says the third.

"Ohhhhhhh, how frustrating", exclaims Santa.

"I specifically asked the employment agency for three ELVES ..."

**10 December 2013** – 13 likes and 1 share

Though others have begun to question the fact, I am pretty convinced that Father Christmas IS a man ...

... what self-respecting woman would wear the same outfit every year??

**11 December 2013** – 9 likes and a share

I recommended a book to my daughter, pointing out that it was a real page turner.

Her response?

'Dad, I know how books work!'

**12 December 2013** – 15 likes

Q. What is the difference between a knight (probably called George) and one of Father Christmas' reindeer (probably not)?
A. One slays the dragon, the other's draggin' the sleigh ...

**13 December 2013** – AMG's birthday

**Simon Gibson**
December 13, 2013

Middle child, number two daughter, has a birthday today. Hope she likes her present ...

Last week I asked her what she wanted for her big day - I think she has been coached by her Mum.

'Thanks for asking, Dad' she said.

'Just give me something with diamonds' ...

... and that is why I am giving her a pack of playing cards.

HAPPY BIRTHDAY x

Like · Comment · Promote · Share

Alwyn Robinson, Margaret Baxter, Janet Hawson and 11 others like this.

**Mark Ashpole** Sounds like a fair deal .......
December 13, 2013 at 8:54am via mobile · Unlike · 👍 1

**Morwenna Clarke** Happy Birthday young lady!!!
December 13, 2013 at 11:42am · Unlike · 👍 1

## 14 December 2013 – 15 likes

More news from the big man –
apparently, some of Santa's helpers
are looking a bit portly, chubby,
somewhat overweight – not to worry,
there is time to go before the big
day, so it's off to the elf farm.

Yes, he provides them with numerous
benefits, including private elf care ...
especially helpful for the short,
depressed one – that's right ... low elf-esteem.

Fisher

## 15 December 2013 – 11 likes

Apparently, before he hired the reindeer, Father Christmas used
dromedaries – they were reliable, happy and always successful. They had
to be replaced when one year they flew over Bethlehem, liked the look of
it and stayed there.

I found this little known fact in a popular tune, often sung at this time of
year – can't believe no-one else spotted it before me:

Oh, camel, ye faithful, joyful and triumphant ...

## 16 December 2013 – 16 likes

Doctor Dickens: What seems to be the trouble?

Patient Scrooge: I have terrible wind and really bad indigestion.

Doctor: What have you been eating?

Patient: You know I like my Italian food – I had macaroni cheese for lunch
yesterday, then lasagne for dinner and spaghetti bolognese today – why?

Doctor: I warned you before that would come back to haunt you.

Patient: So you mean to say ...

Doctor: Yes, it's the ghost of Christmas Pasta ...

**17 December 2013** – 15 likes

Some of you make your own crackers (and your own punchlines!) so for the next three days ...

Q. Who can you find hiding in the bakers at Christmas?
A. The mince spy.

**18 December 2013** – 16 likes

Crackers, 2 of 3:
Q. What do you call an old snowman?
A. Water.

**19 December 2013** – 13 likes

Crackers, 3 of 3:
Q. What do you have in December that you don't get in any other month?

A. D.

**20 December 2013** – 18 likes

We were out walking with friends the other day – me, my wife, our French friend Claude, Rudolph (he's Russian) and their wives. It looked as if we might be in for some poor whether (also known as a bad spell of weather) ...

I said I was sure we would just get a few spots of rain, and that it would soon be dry again. Claude was convinced that we would get all hell break loose (he's a bit like Satan, Claude).

My wife said we should ask Rudolph's opinion, so we did.

He said it would rain heavily for 17 minutes, then slow to a light drizzle for nine minutes, at which point we'd see a rainbow just as the sun came out, and it would then be dry.

Amazingly, that is EXACTLY what happened!

I asked my wife how she was so confident about our Russian friend and this special ability. 'Oh', she replied, 'I thought everyone knew ...

... Rudolph the red knows rain, dear.'

## 21 December 2013 – 11 likes

Today, we eavesdrop on a group therapy session, just before Christmas, where Santa, a snowman and Rudolph (yes, the red-nose reindeer again) are all discussing their problems:

Santa – I find it hard to believe in myself.
Snowman – I think I might be bi-polar.
Rudolph – all the other reindeer laugh and call me names!

## 22 December 2013 – 13 likes

On Friday, my wife gave me a heavy hint about what she hopes to get for Christmas.

'I'd really like cutting edge technology', she revealed.
Don't tell her, but I think I've nailed it – I have bought her ...

... a cordless electric hedge trimmer.

## 23 December 2013 – 7 likes

I was looking for a turkey at the weekend and went to the supermarket – I found one, not really big enough for what I need.

'Excuse me', I asked the assistant. 'Do these turkeys get any bigger.'

'No', came the reply. 'They're dead'.

Somewhat put out, and needing something else for the Christmas table, I went to see the butcher next and asked if he had a capon.

'Who do you think I am?', he asked. 'Batman?'

## 24 December 2013 – 12 likes and lots of sympathy!

Husband (definition): a man who orders and pays for his tickets for the whole football season three months before the first match, buys enough beer/wine for (at least) a month at a time, knows when his next 'surprise, last minute' night out 'with the boys' is six weeks ahead of time ...

... and buys his Christmas presents on Christmas Eve!
(Apparently)

**25 December 2013** – 3 today – first, 7 likes

Christmas trilogy – humour, rhyme, humour – now only six days to go:

Part I

Huge excitement last night, as we anticipated the arrival of the main man.

Eventually, having seen the children off to sleep, I went to bed in the fireplace. It worked – I slept like a log!

Then – 16 likes:

Part the second

Every year at this very time
I celebrate Christmas in rhyme
Among all the banter
We wait, just for Santa
To celebrate something sublime

The children of course love it most
Awaiting their cards in the post...
Though now they all get
Mainly via internet
But some things don't change, like the roast

The turkey's the usual choice
Nowadays paid via invoice
Then at round about three
It's The Queen, and then tea
After supper, we all find our voice

By the end of the day we are spent
Religion is over 'til Lent
Though just a week on
We party on and on
As the New Year is quite an event

Today leaves me just six more days
Of my jokes, that have left some in haze
It has been really great
Posted often 'fore 8
Your support I can really just praise

**Then** – 11 likes:

Part III

Dr., Dr., I am afraid of Father Christmas!

That's OK, you're just Claus-trophobic.

**26 December 2013** – 15 likes

Woops! Just found out one of my younger colleagues bought his girlfriend a pair of goalies gloves for Christmas ...

... just because after I met her at the staff party I told him I thought she was a keeper ...

**27 December 2013** – 15 likes

Post-Christmas, it turns out I don't need to go on a diet at all – my weight is perfect.

I just happen to be 2 feet too short ...

**28 December 2013** – 11 likes

Q. What did the reindeer get for Christmas?
A. A pony sleigh station ...

(one for the youngsters ...)

**29 December 2013** – 20 likes

Spending time at home means I can do all those jobs that keep being put off

Yesterday, I went to the local curtain store to get a curtain rod, and the manager asked me how long I'd like it.

I said, 'I'd quite like to keep it' ...

## 30 December 2013 – 14 likes

About this time last year I recall my wife was taking an afternoon nap, having been tired out by Christmas and before the New Year festivities got into full swing.

After she woke up, she told me, "I just dreamed that you gave me a diamond ring for a New Year's present. What do you think that means?"

"Ah, you'll know tomorrow," I answered, cryptically.

At midnight the next day, as the New Year came in, I approached my wife and handed her a small package. Clearly excited, she opened it quickly.

There in her hand rested a book entitled, "Interpreting the meaning of dreams."

## 31 December 2013 – that's all folks!! – 28 likes and lots of lovely comments …

So, my other brother, George, is a bit of a marketing genius – the bright one in the family. He is also very well qualified, as both a Veterinary and a Taxidermist. His business cards are quite something – they state:

His name;
His qualifications;
His address;
His email, Twitter and telephone details;
His website; and finally …
… his marketing strap line …

… which is …

'Whatever happens, you get your dog back!'

**Mark Ashpole** Simon, A huge well done to you for completing your AjokeAday challenge, raising funds and awareness for such a fantastic cause. Thank you for making a difference. Mark A
December 31, 2013 at 8:22am via mobile · Unlike · 👍 1

**Katy Baxter** Classic! Well done Simon! Happy New Year xx
December 31, 2013 at 8:23am via mobile · Unlike · 👍 1

**Elaine Milne** And I'm still awake for 365! Happy New Year! 😃
December 31, 2013 at 8:26am via mobile · Unlike · 👍 2

**Anthony Jones** Fabulous , huge congratulations .
December 31, 2013 at 8:31am · Unlike · 👍 1

**Rachel Levitt** A fitting end. Well done.
December 31, 2013 at 8:32am via mobile · Unlike · 👍 1

**Ian Green** I've been waiting all year for this one!
December 31, 2013 at 8:46am via mobile · Unlike · 👍 3

**Margaret Baxter** Amazing achievement! Very well done Simon, a Happy New Year and all the best with the book! xx
December 31, 2013 at 8:49am via mobile · Unlike · 👍 1

**David Braithwaite** Brilliant joke and great achievement overall.
December 31, 2013 at 9:09am via mobile · Unlike · 👍 1

**Morwenna Clarke** ........and relax!!! 😃 CONGRATULATIONS!!
December 31, 2013 at 9:31am via mobile · Unlike · 👍 1

**Julie Gibson** Well done Simon, proud of you. Will miss my monthly chuckle! X
December 31, 2013 at 12:34pm via mobile · Unlike · 👍 1

**Melissa Reddell** Saving the best joke til last! Happy New year xx
December 31, 2013 at 1:17pm via mobile · Unlike · 👍 1

**Bhupinder Anand** Ending with a cracker - could have been placed in one! Well done Simon, thank you for the daily smile!
December 31, 2013 at 1:55pm via mobile · Unlike · 👍 1

**Paula MacMillan** Congrats Simon and the happiest of new year's wishes from very cold Ccccccanada (-45c with windchill this morning)
December 31, 2013 at 1:56pm via mobile · Unlike · 👍 2

 **Stevie Ray Plewes** A perfect ending.....
December 31, 2013 at 3:11pm via mobile · Unlike · 👍 1

 **Dean Hobbs** I never get bored of that joke 🙂 Congratulations Simon, great achievement. Can't wait for the book. Happy New Year to you and the family
December 31, 2013 at 5:40pm via mobile · Unlike · 👍 1

 **Doug Bennett** Great finale, HNY
December 31, 2013 at 5:51pm · Unlike · 👍 1

 **Sue Hedger** A great achievement and a great cause. Saw Grace (H) yesterday - content and happy as always.
December 31, 2013 at 5:54pm · Unlike · 👍 1

# That's all, folks!